How to DRAW Halloween Stuff

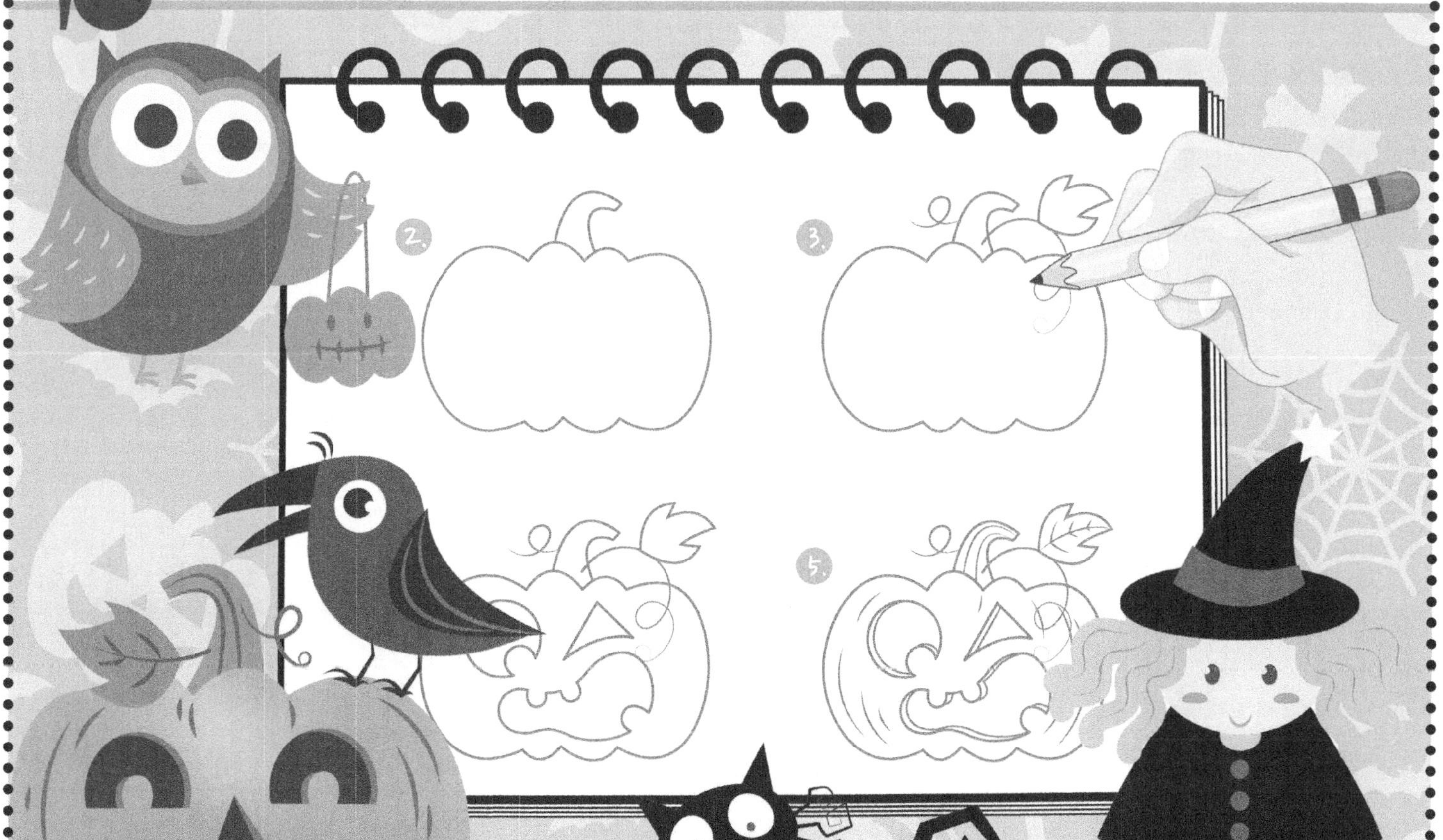

Learn to Draw Cute Halloween Stuff!

Learning to draw doesn't have to be hard. This book will show you how to draw fun Halloween stuff including jack-o-lanterns, witches, ghosts, bats, black cats, spiders, and more.

All you need is a pencil, an eraser, and some paper to get started!

Follow along with each illustration that shows you how to draw step by step. Add each detail as shown until the picture is finished. Start off drawing lightly and don't worry about making mistakes. You can always erase and start over.

When you're finished, you can add your own details and color it!

Let's go!

CUTE PUMPKIN

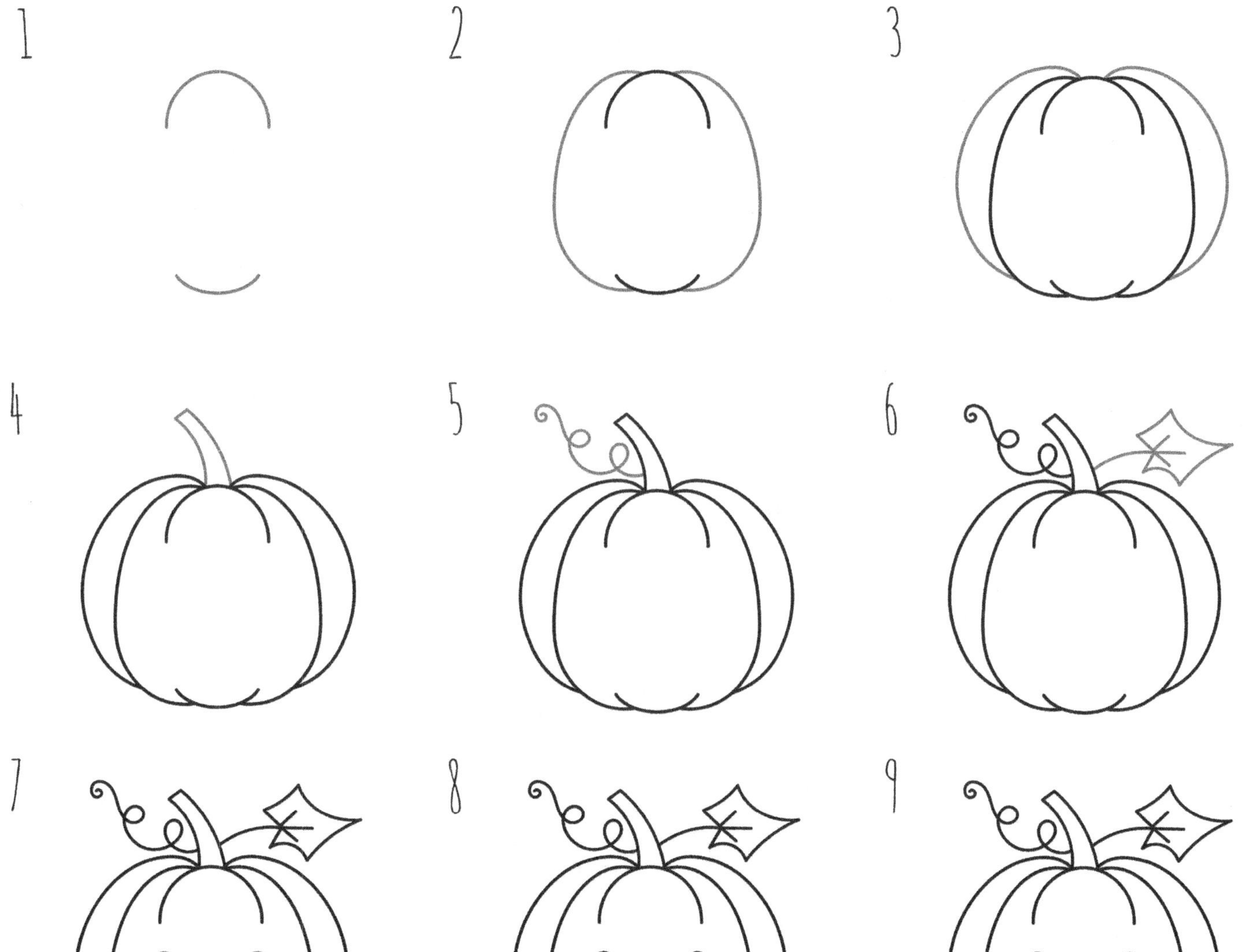

GHOST

1.

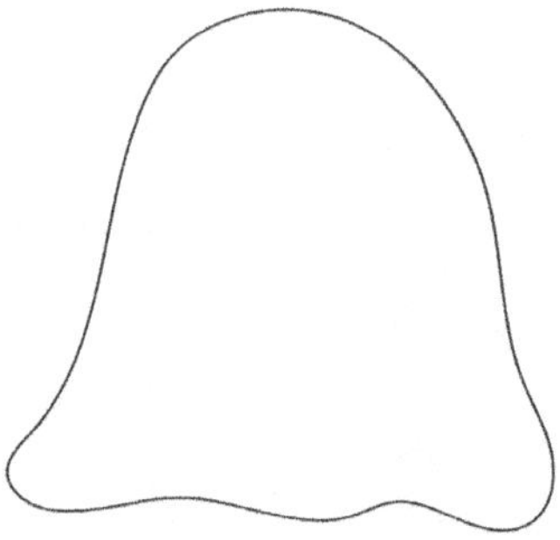

2.

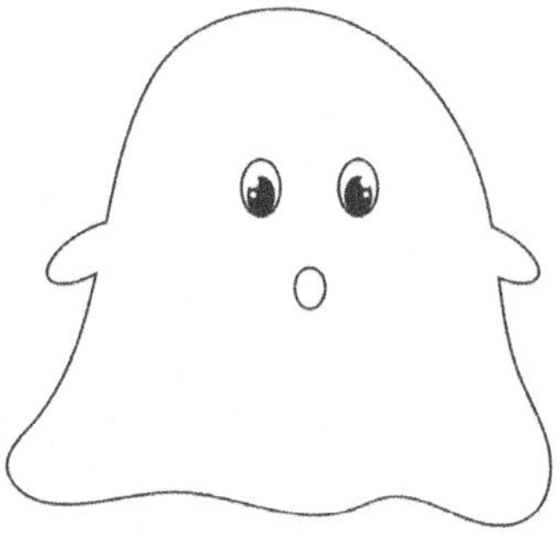

3.

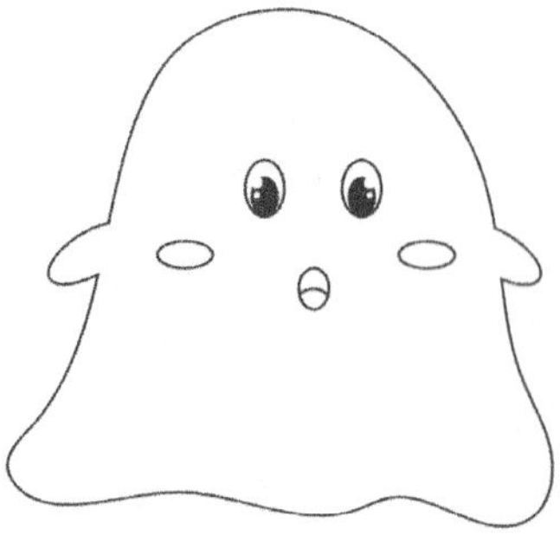

4.

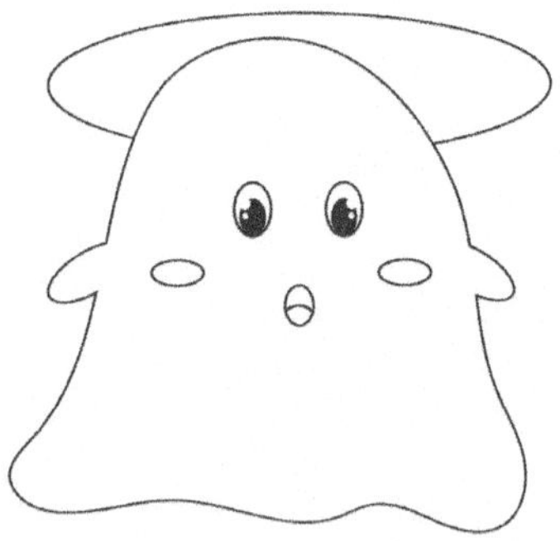

5.

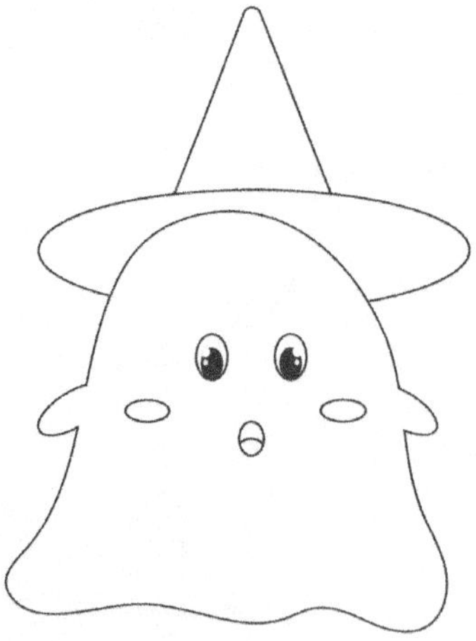

FLYING BAT

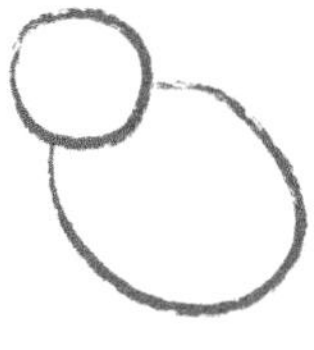

1

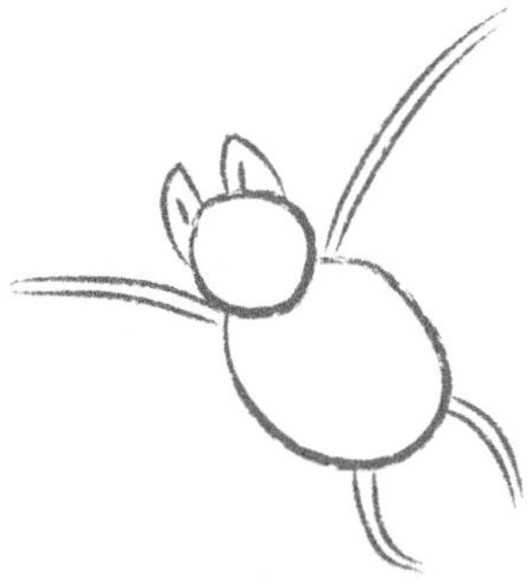

2

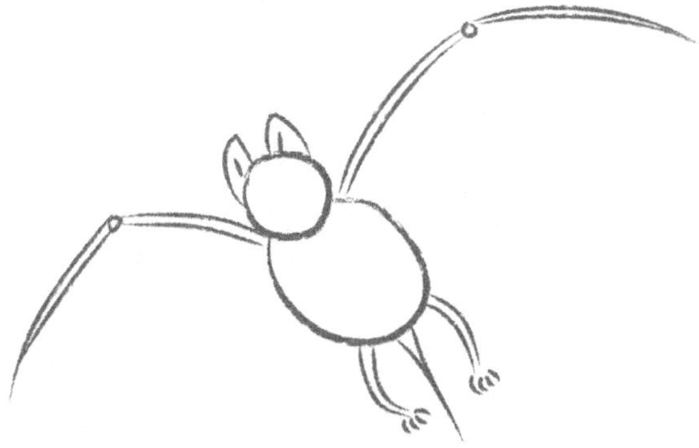

3

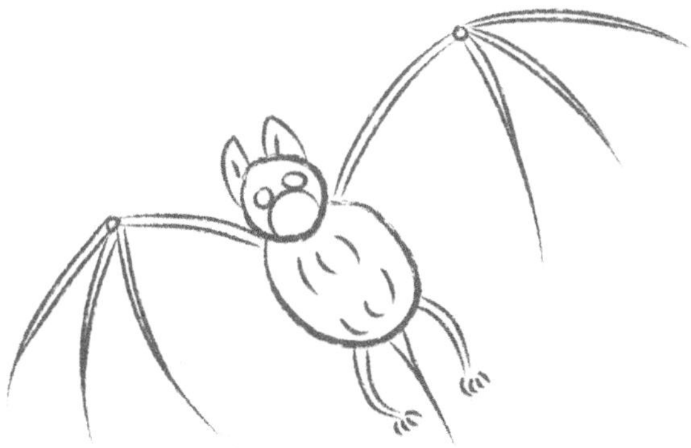

4

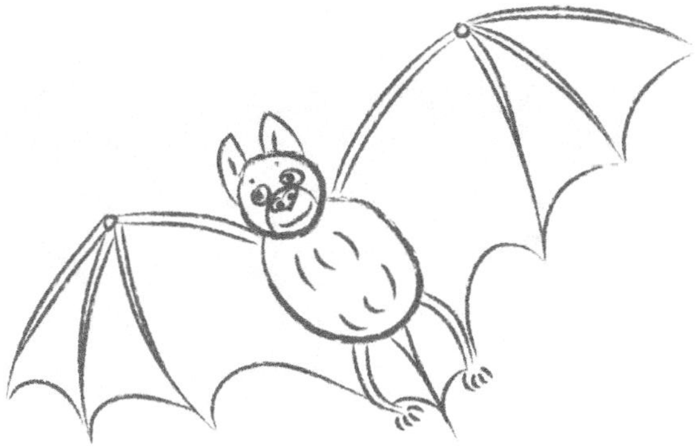

5

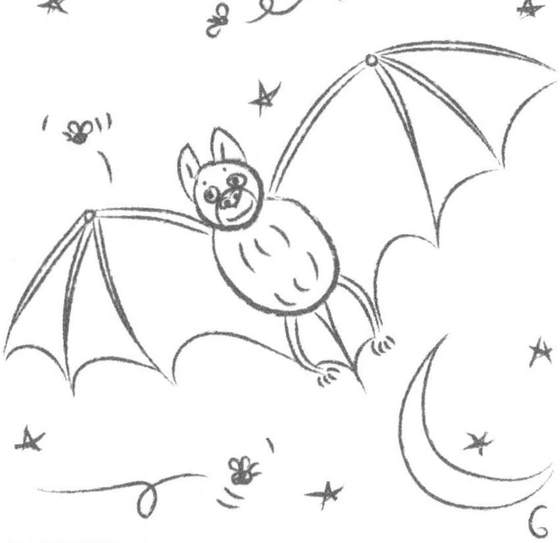

6

SPIDER WEB

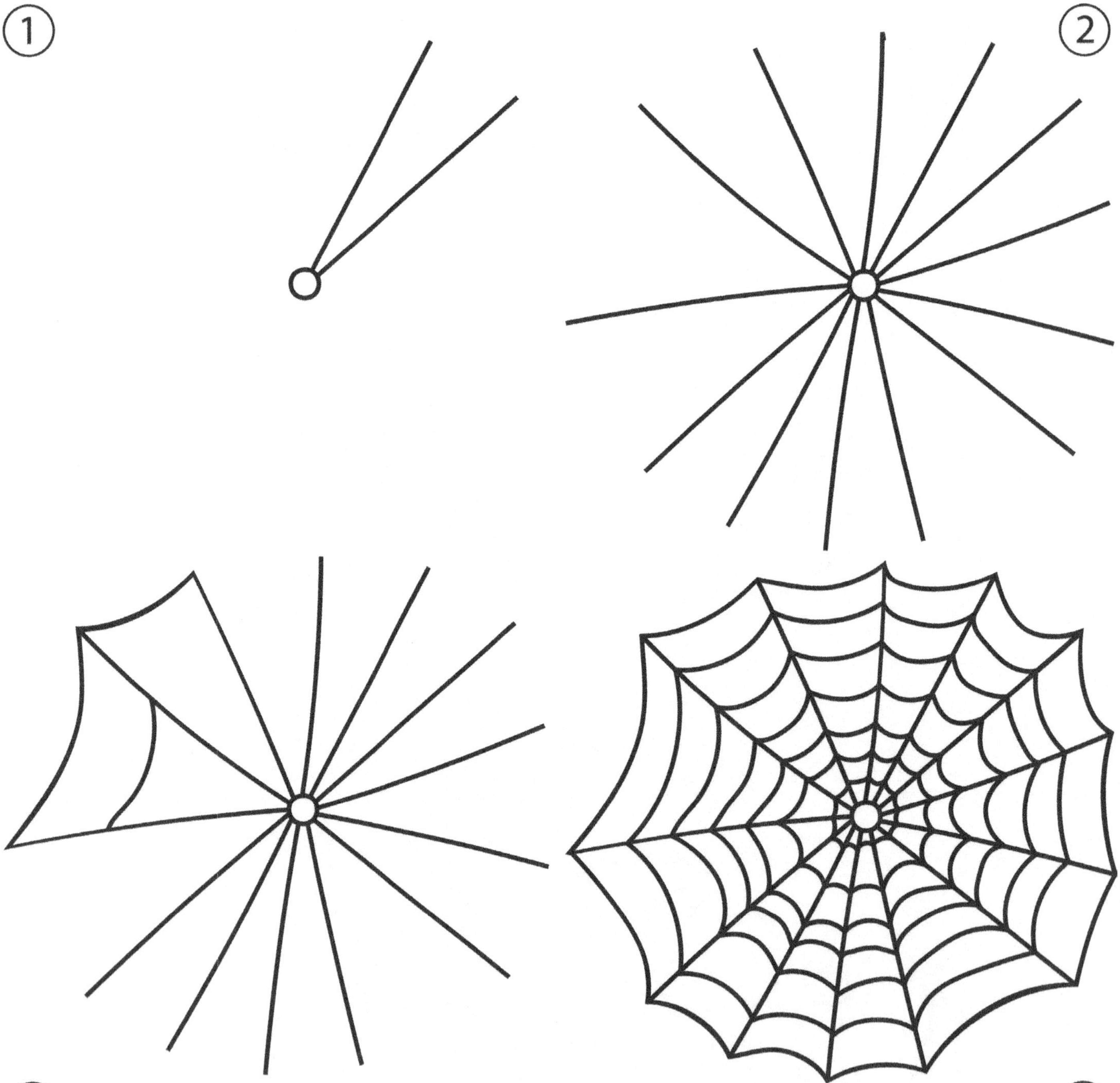

SPIDER

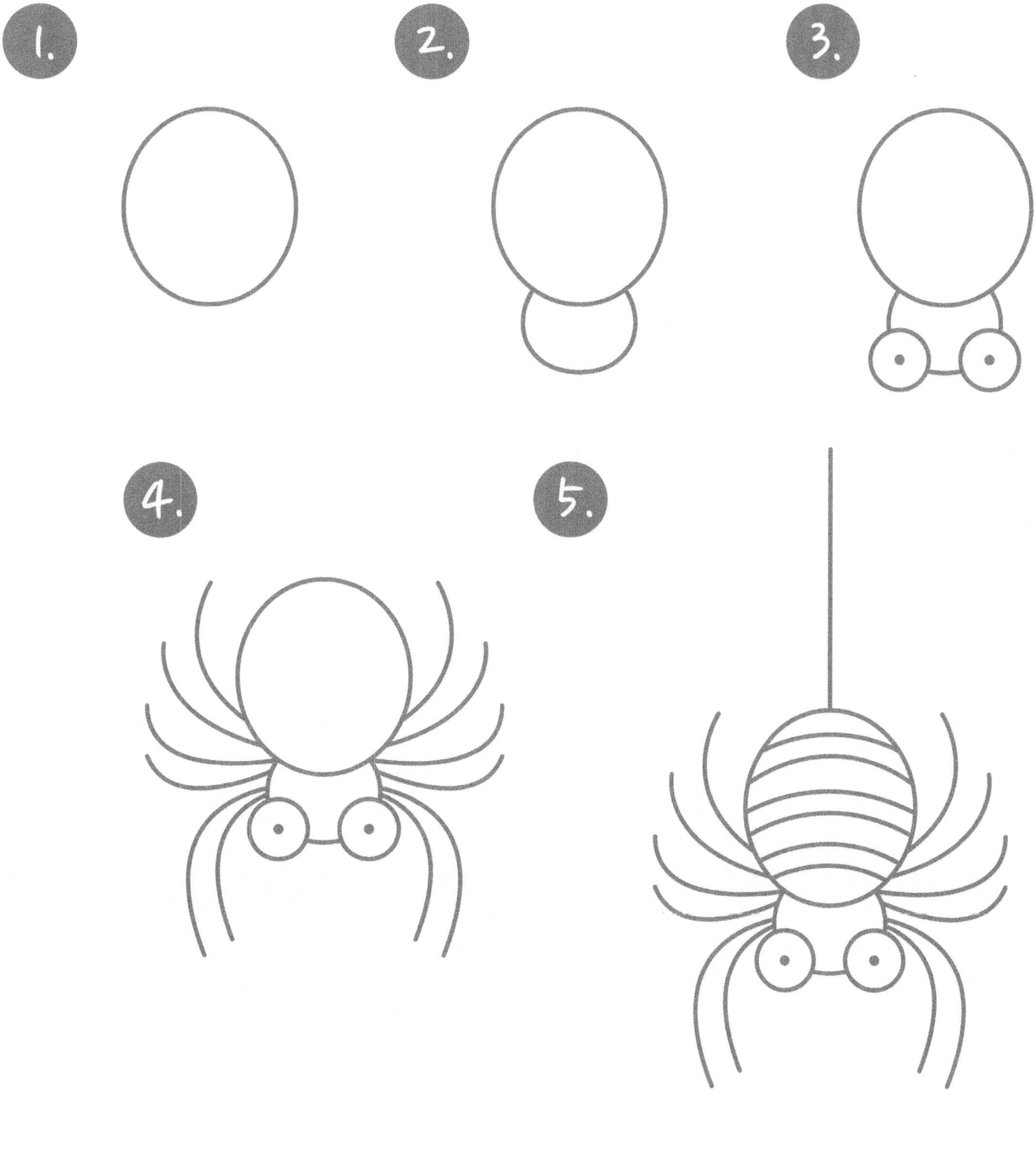

SILLY BAT

1.

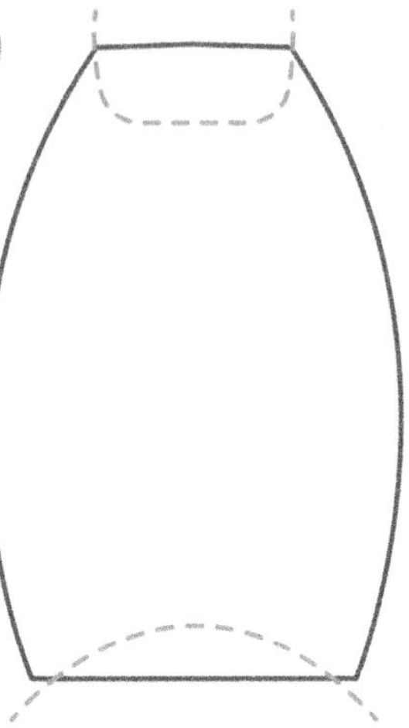

2.

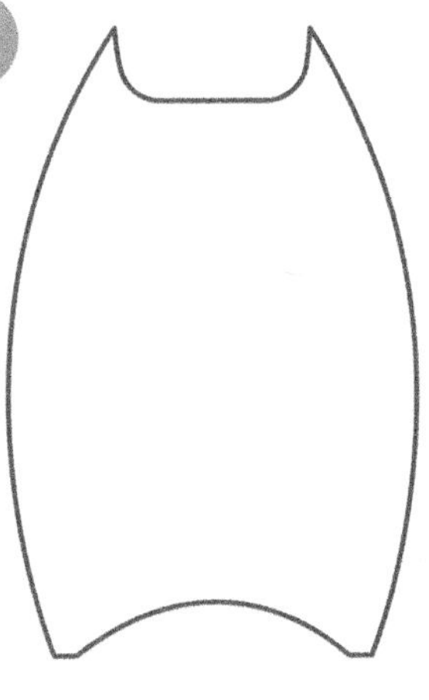

3.

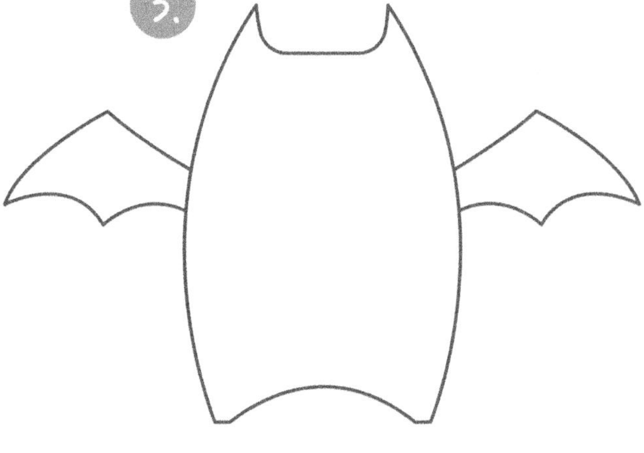

4.

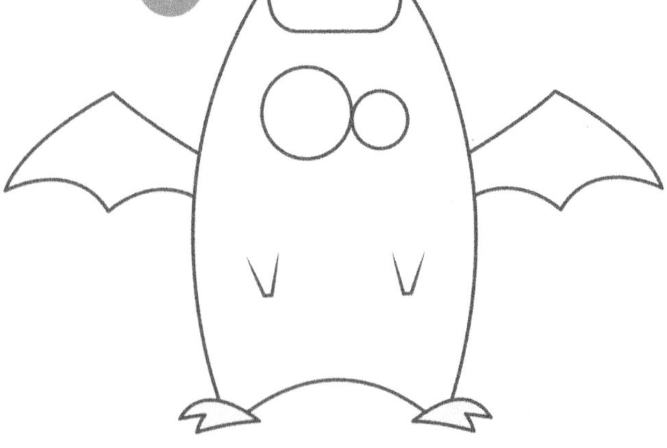

5.

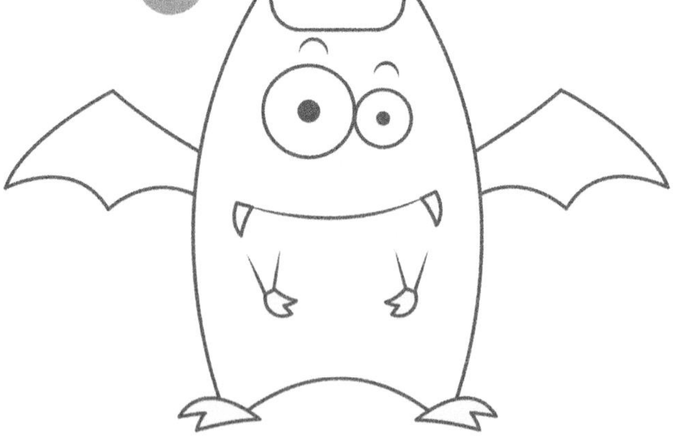

SCAREDY CAT

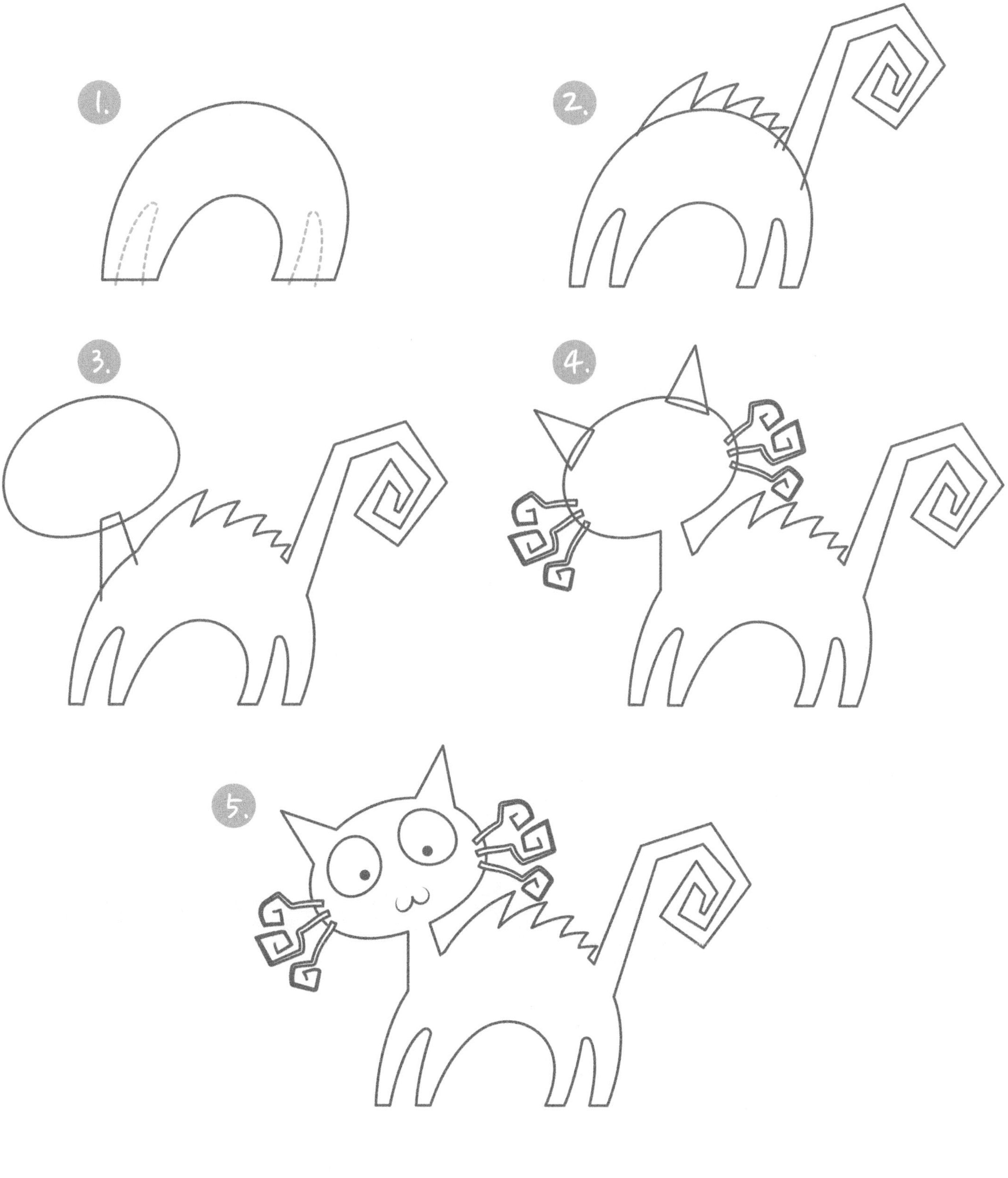

PUMPKIN MAN

1.

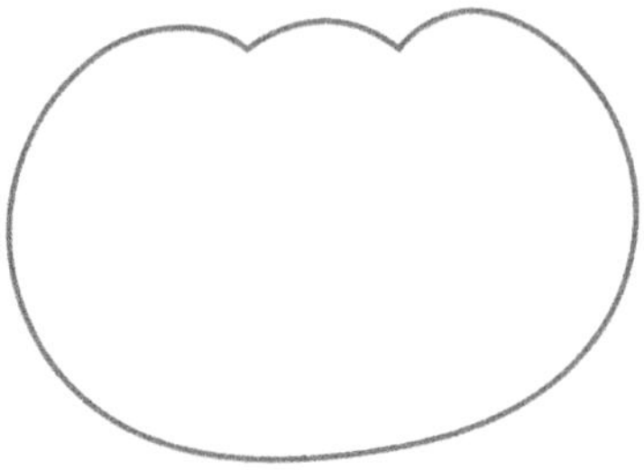

2.

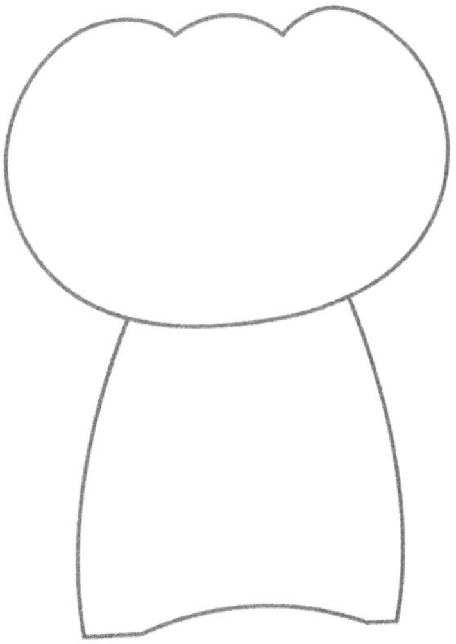

3.

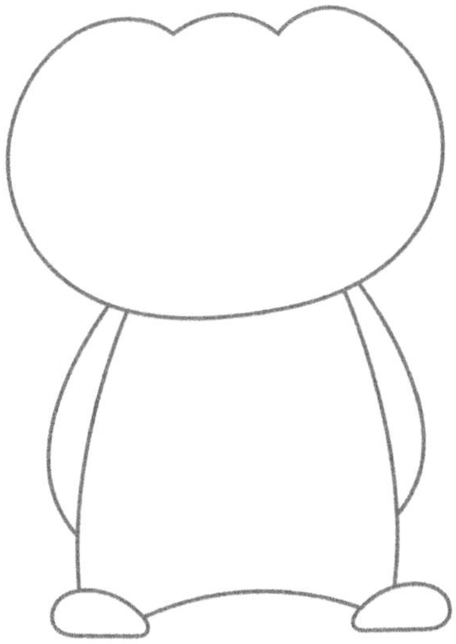

4.

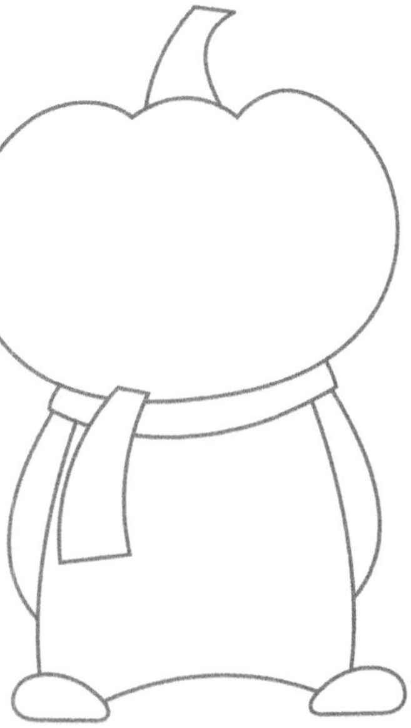

5.

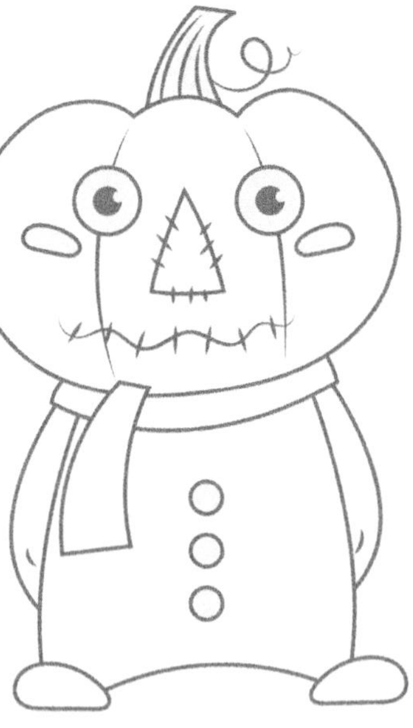

LONG LEGS

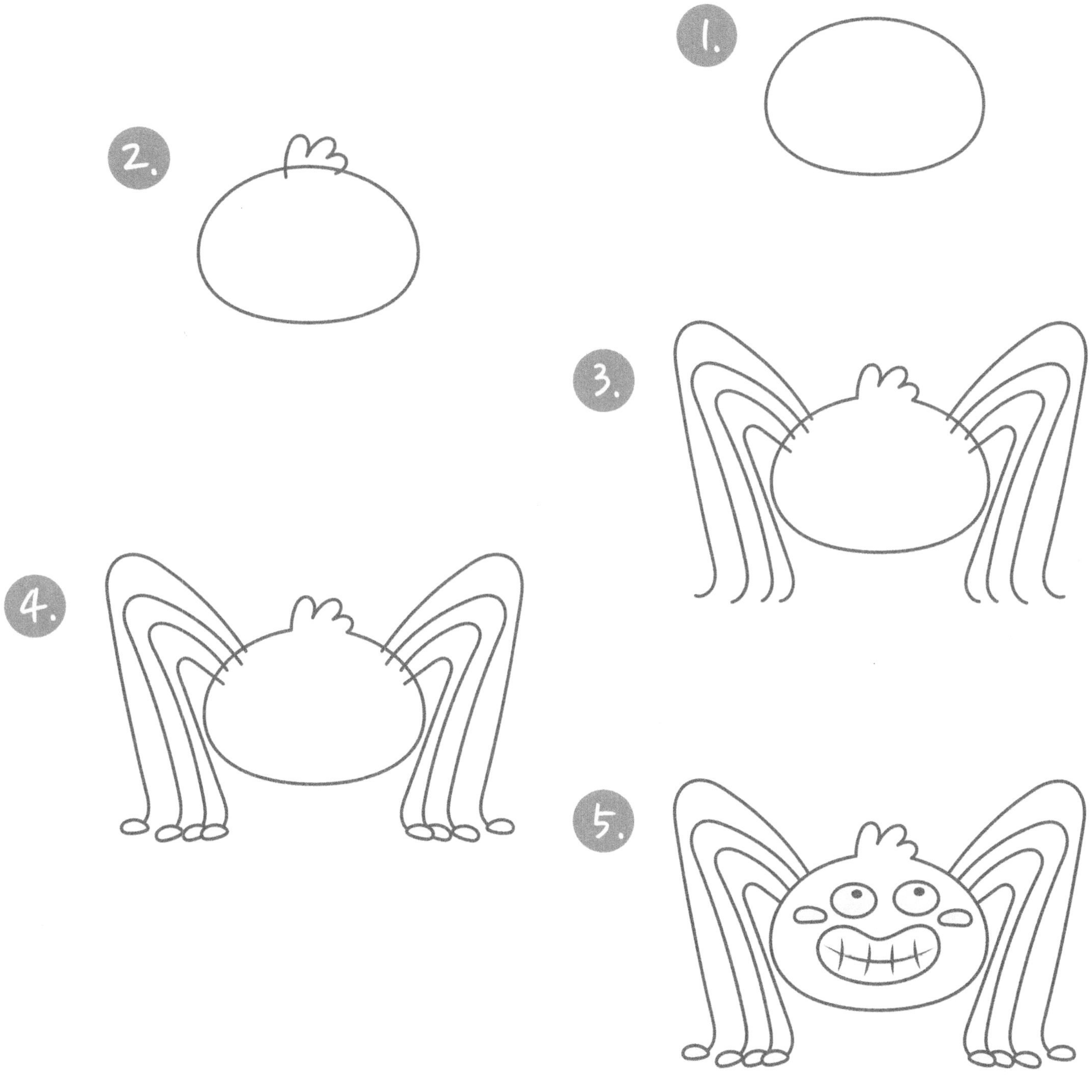

GHOST WITCH

1.

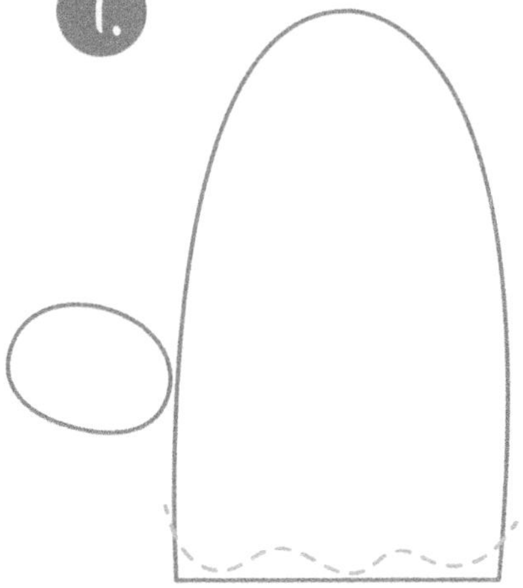

2.

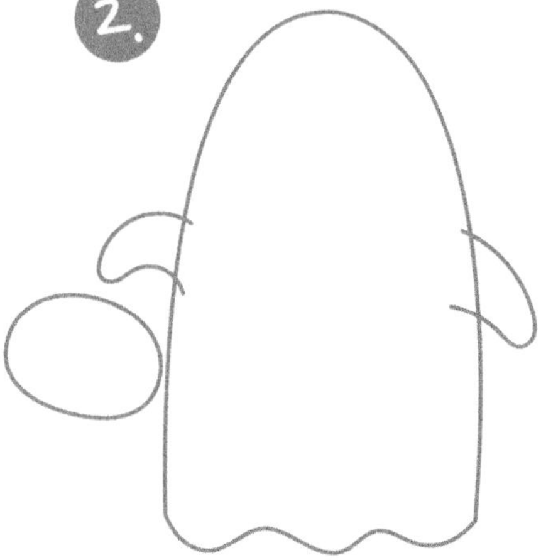

3.

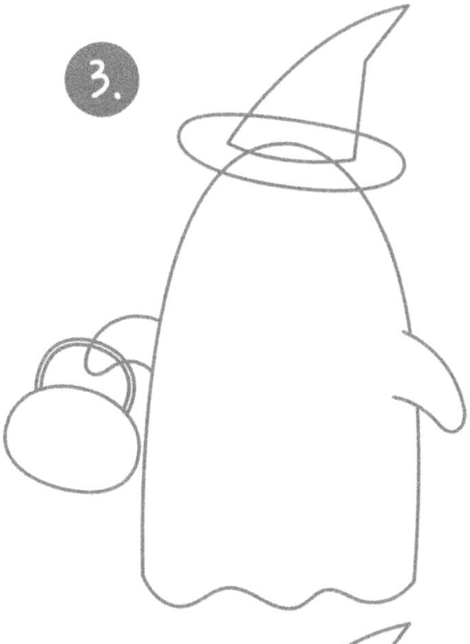

4.

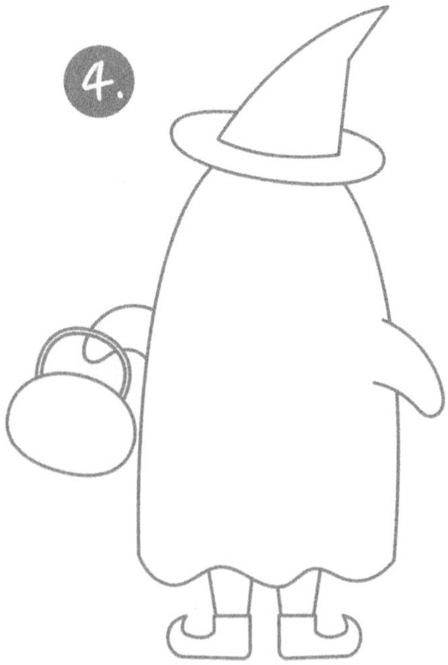

5.

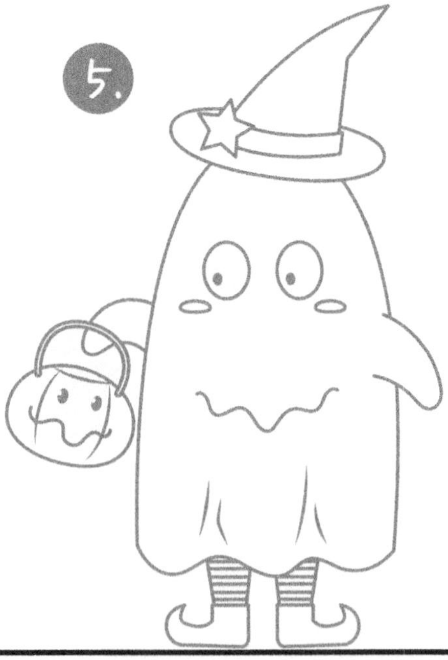

CANDY CORN MAN

1.

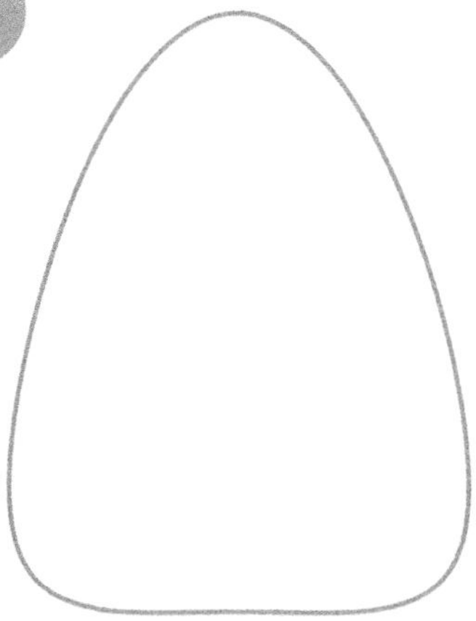

2.

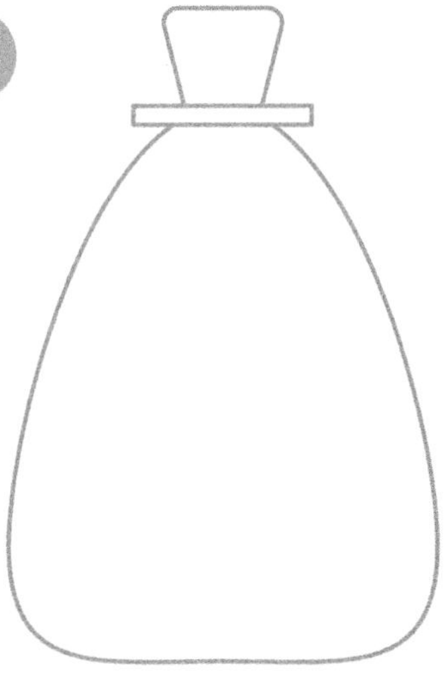

3.

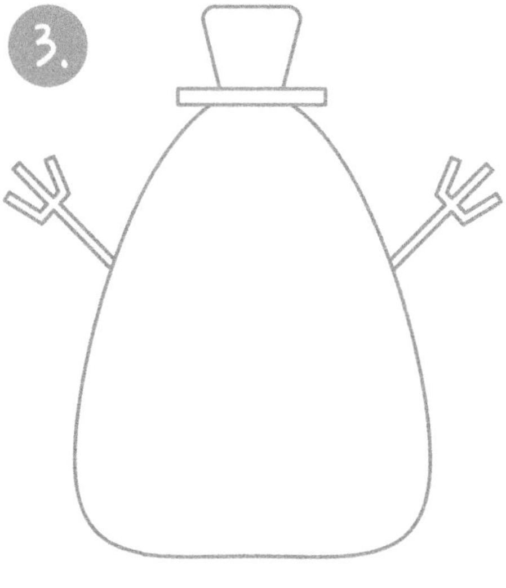

4.

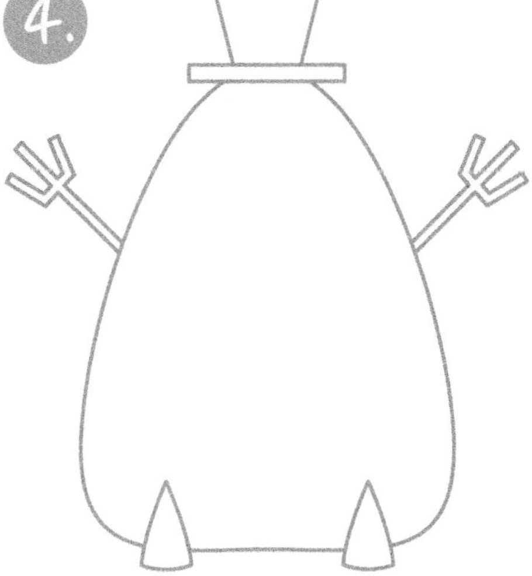

5.

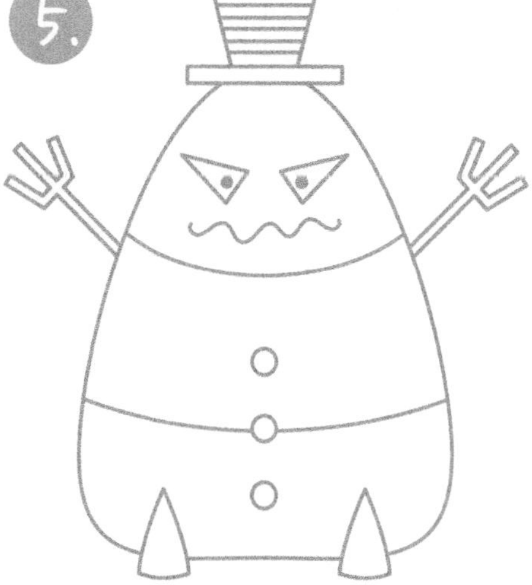

WITCH

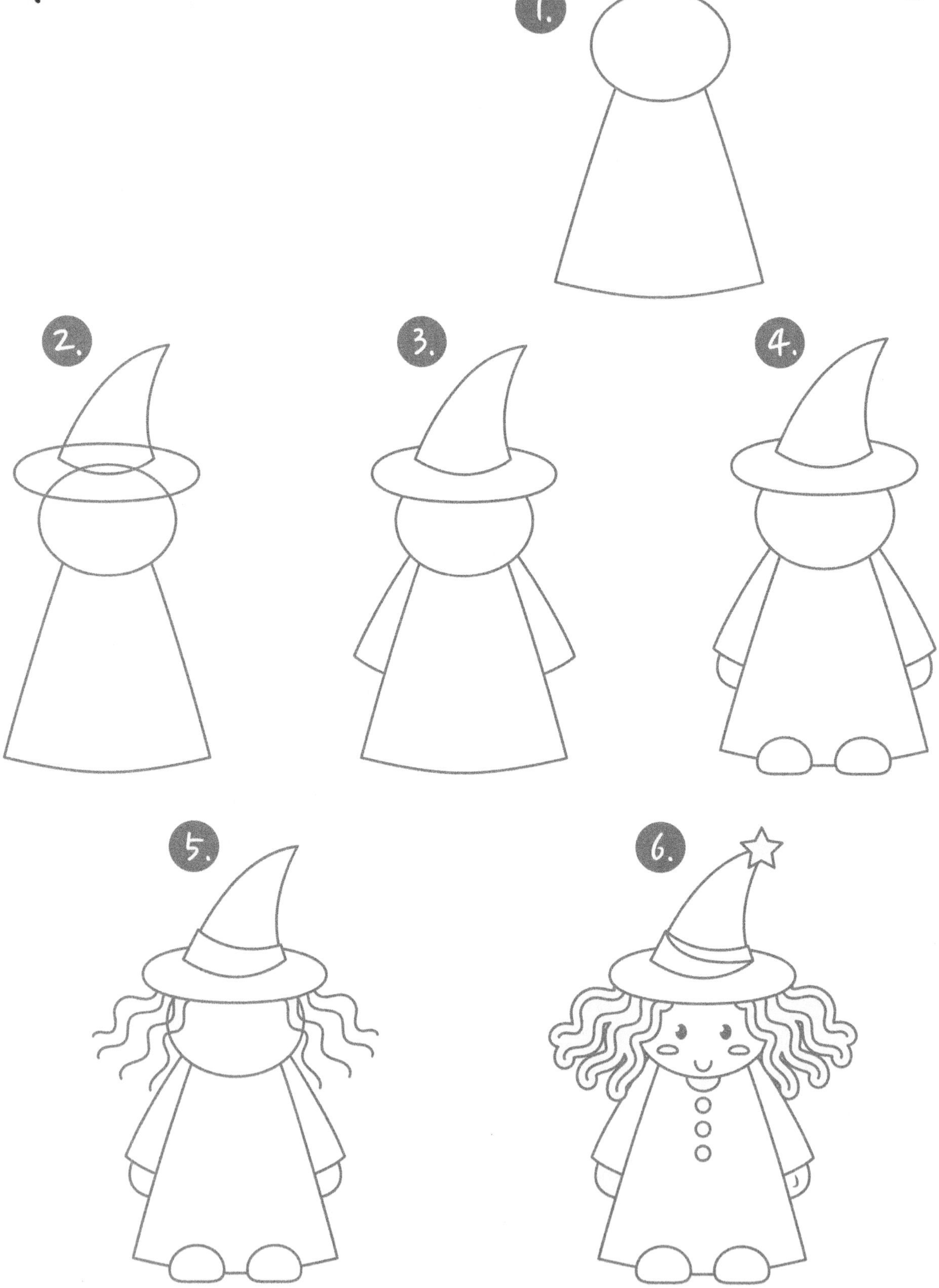

ACORN

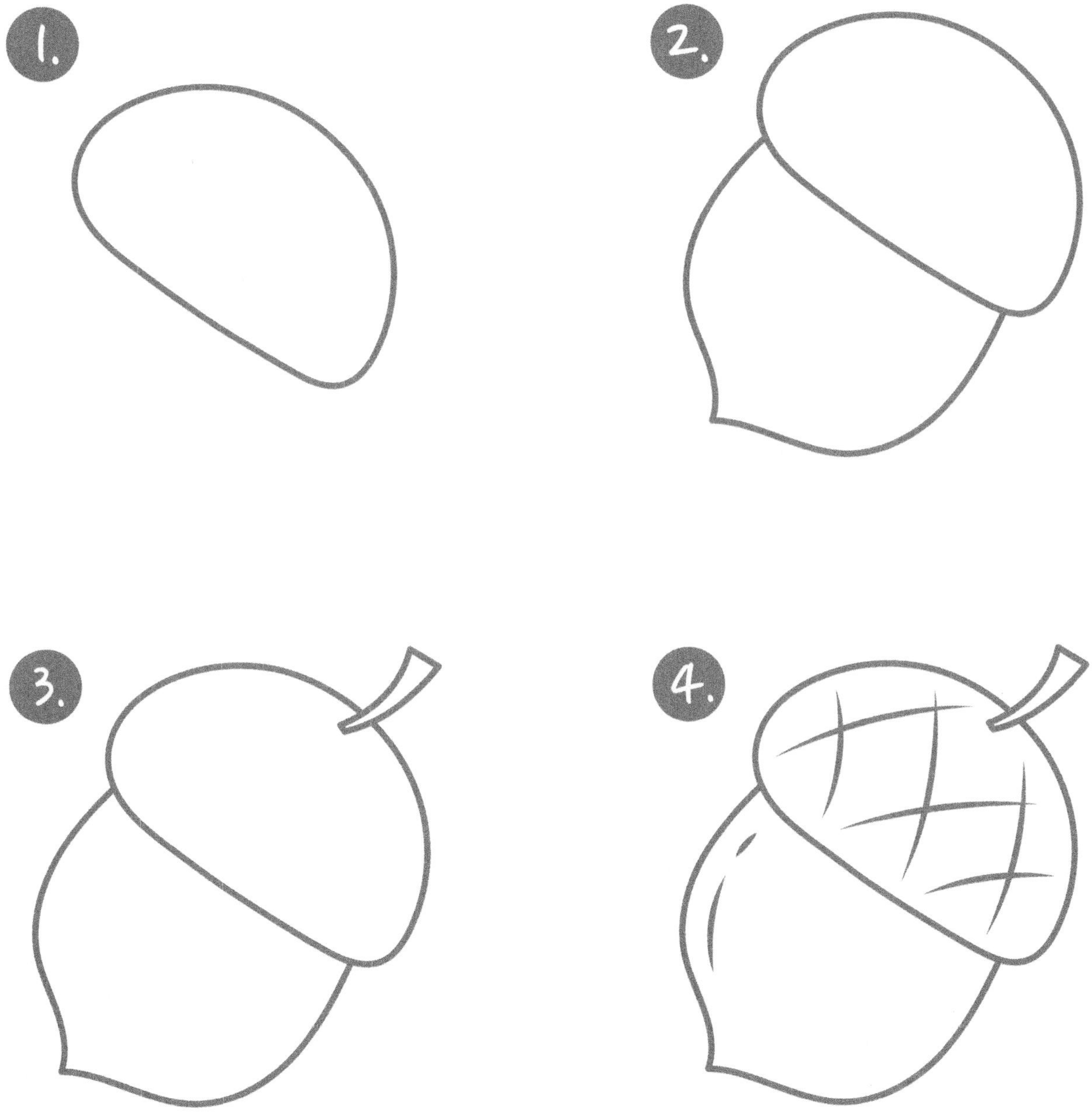

CUPCAKE

JACK-O-LANTERN

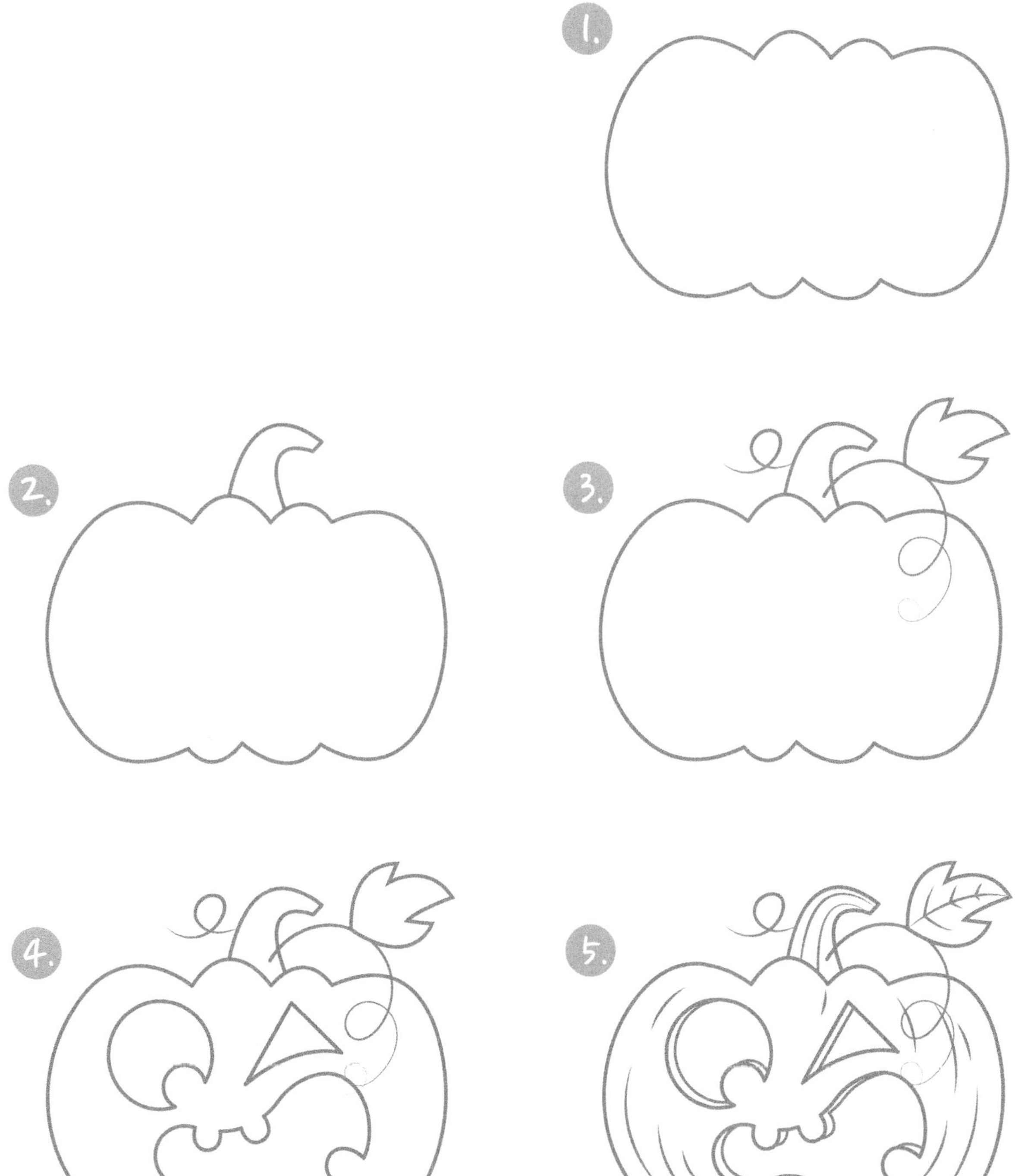

HAPPY CAT

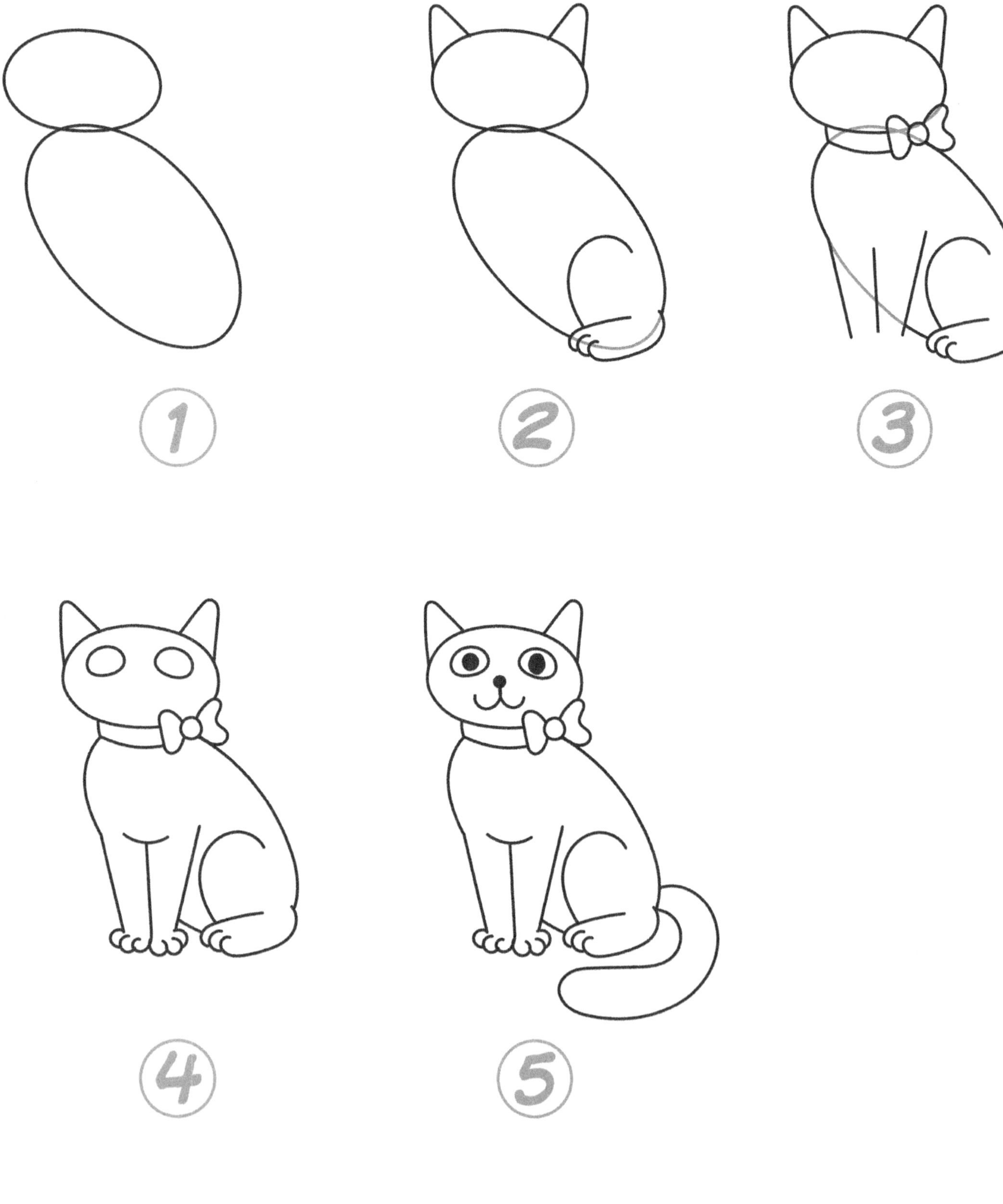

WISE OWL

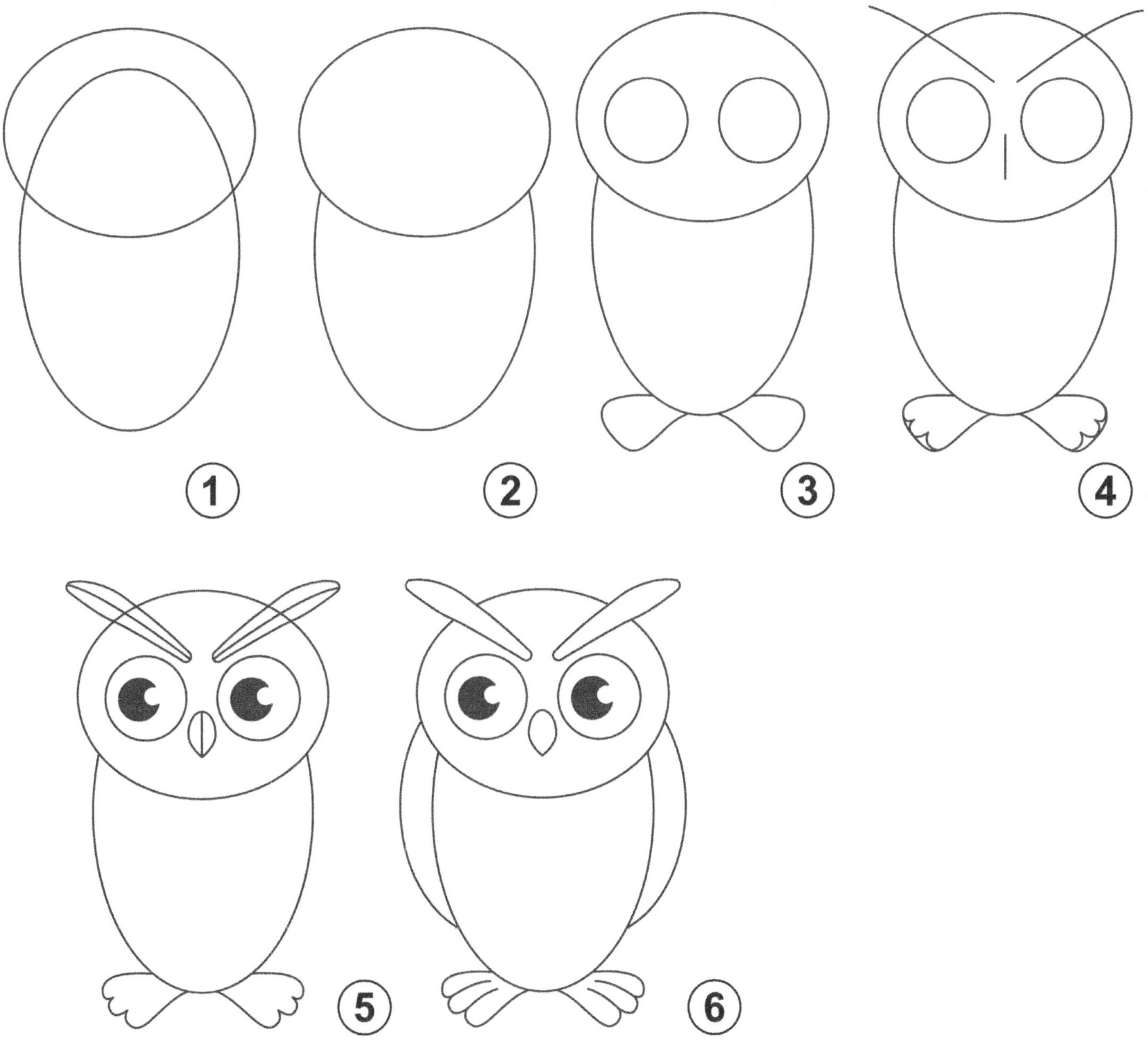

BIRD ON PUMPKIN

1.

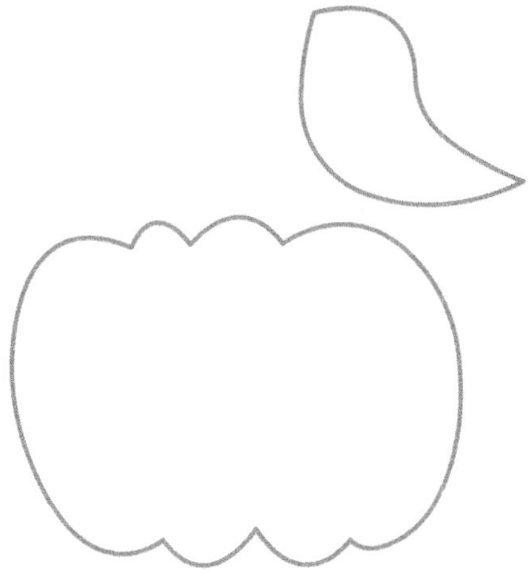

2.

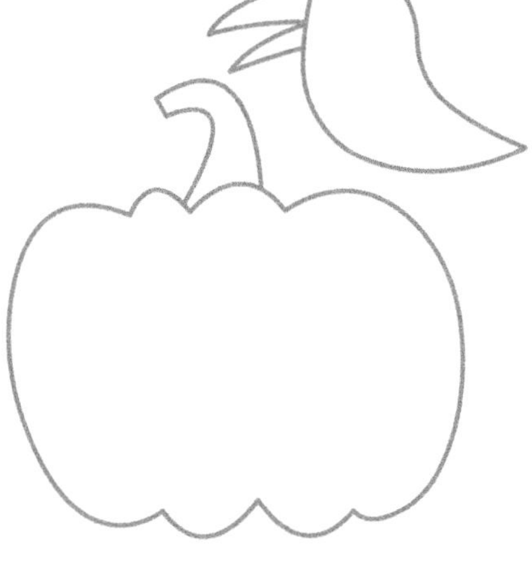

3.

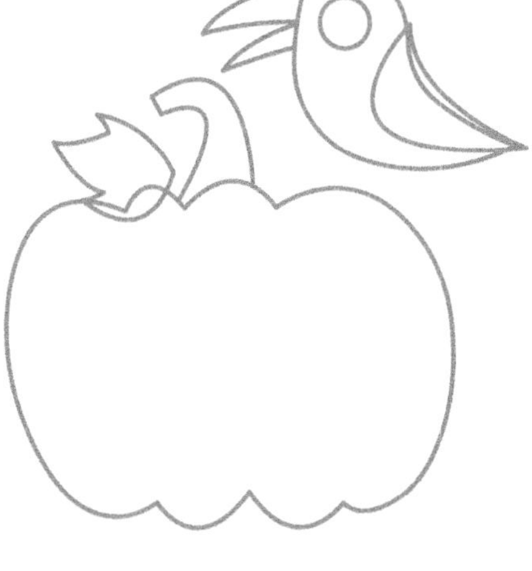

4.

5.

WITCH'S SHOE

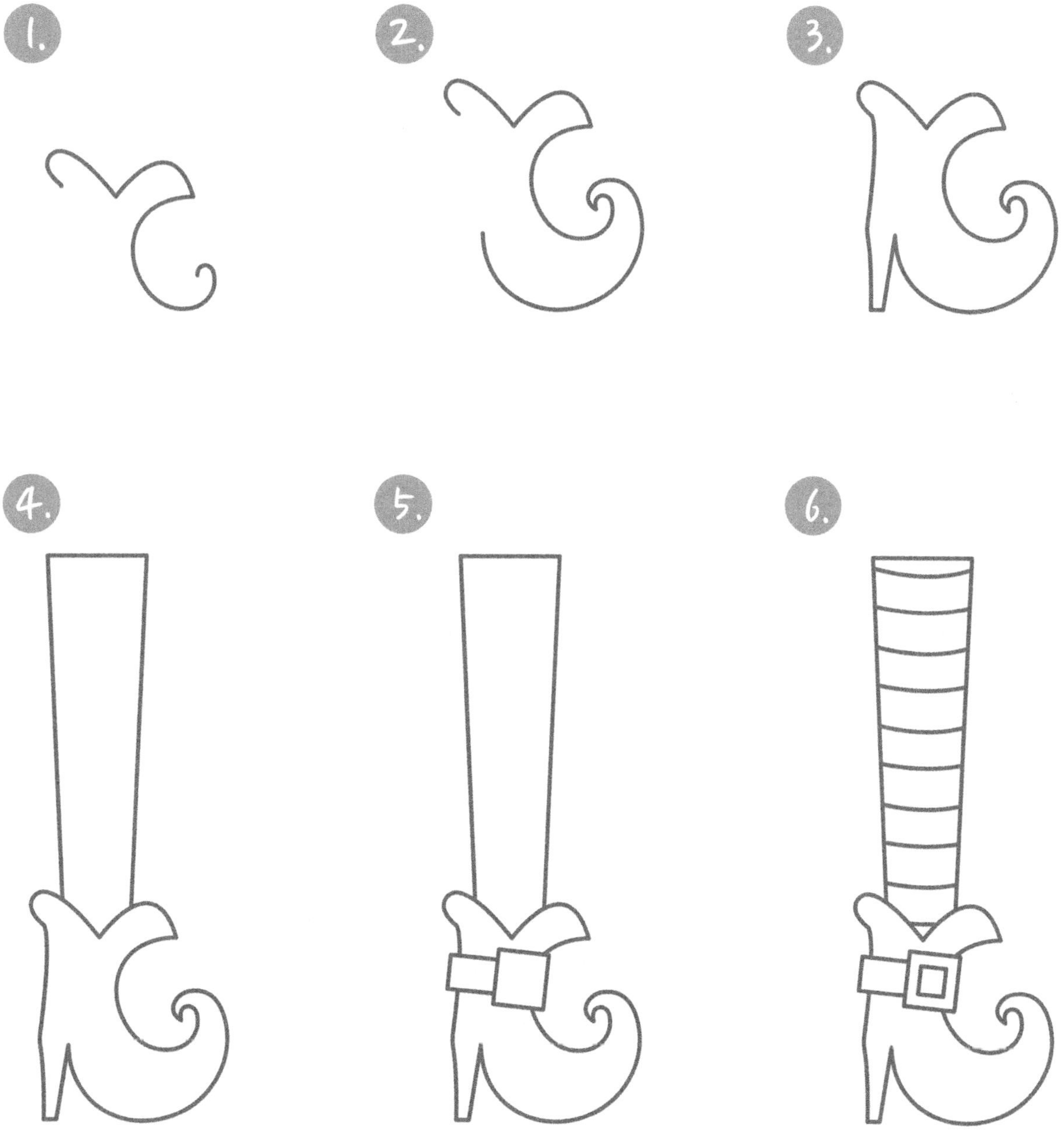

OWL

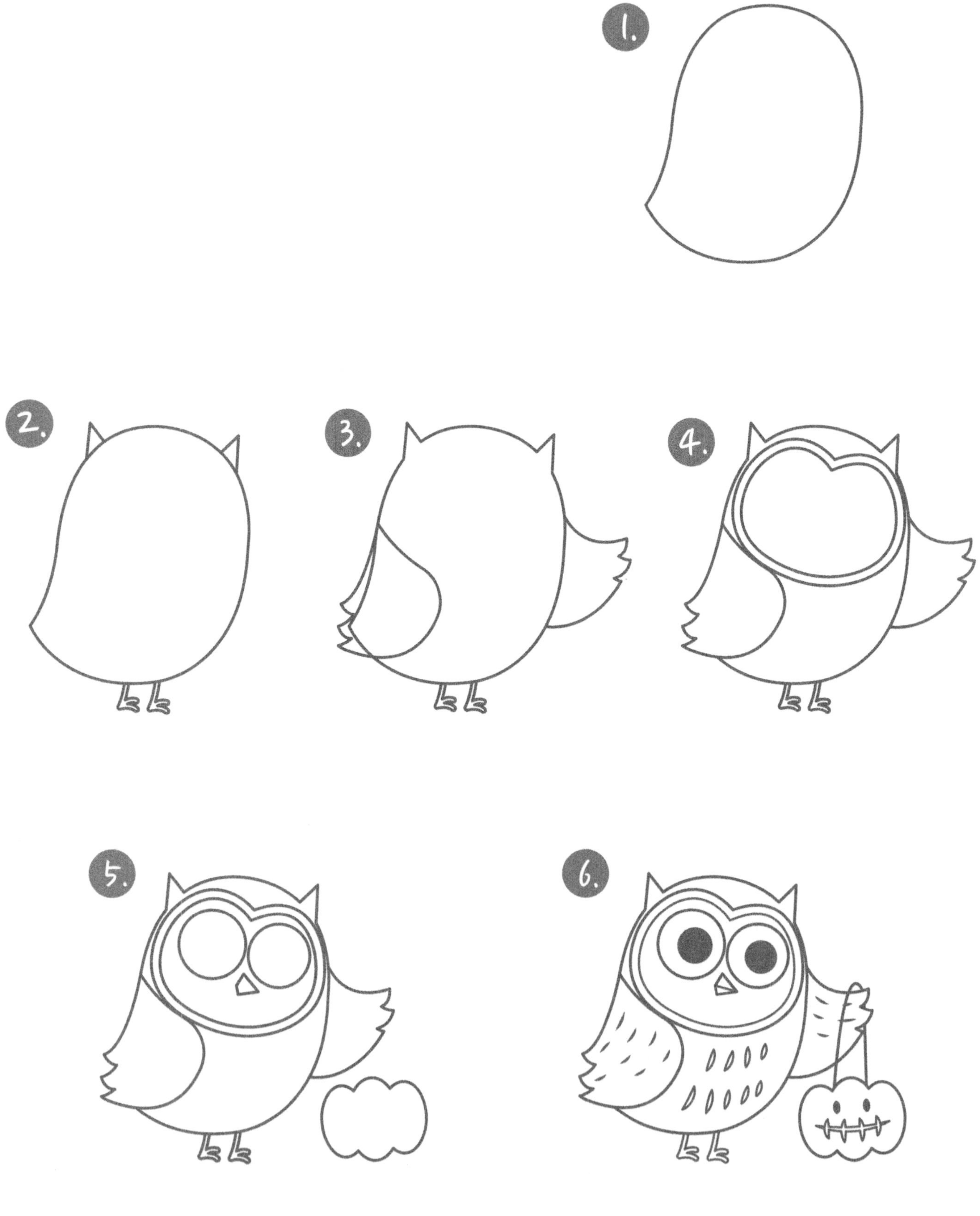

GHOST

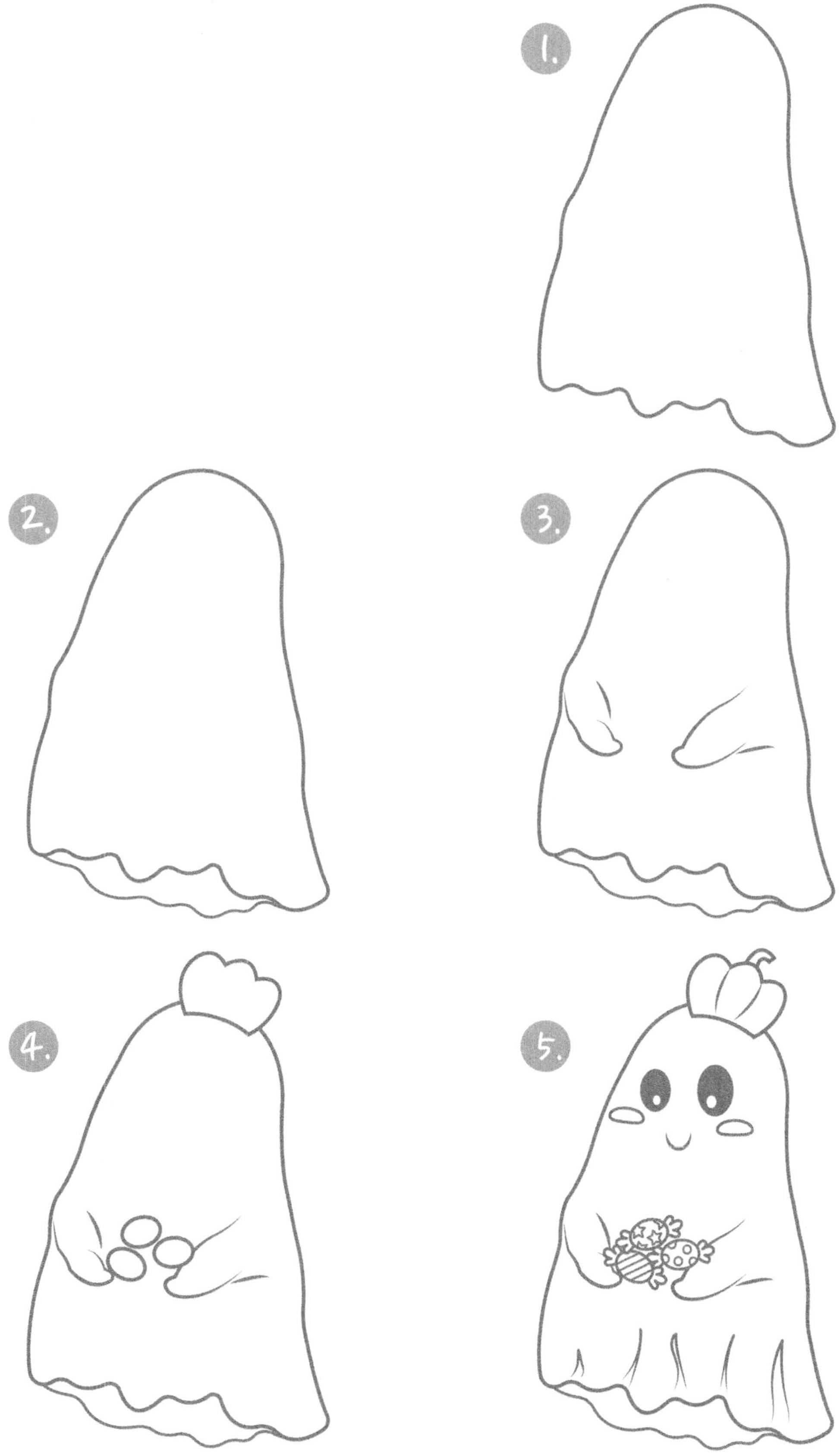

CROW

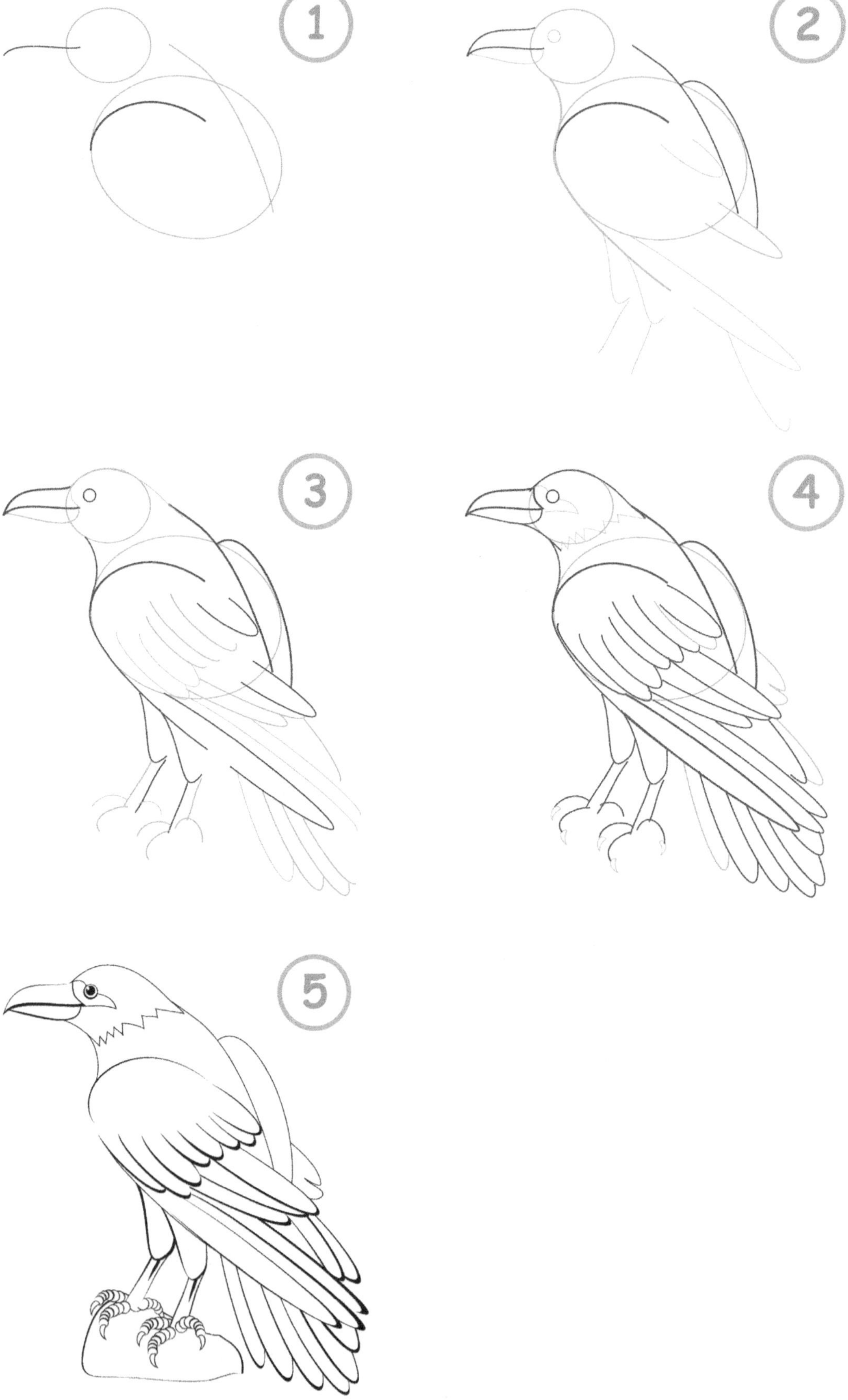

SCARECROW

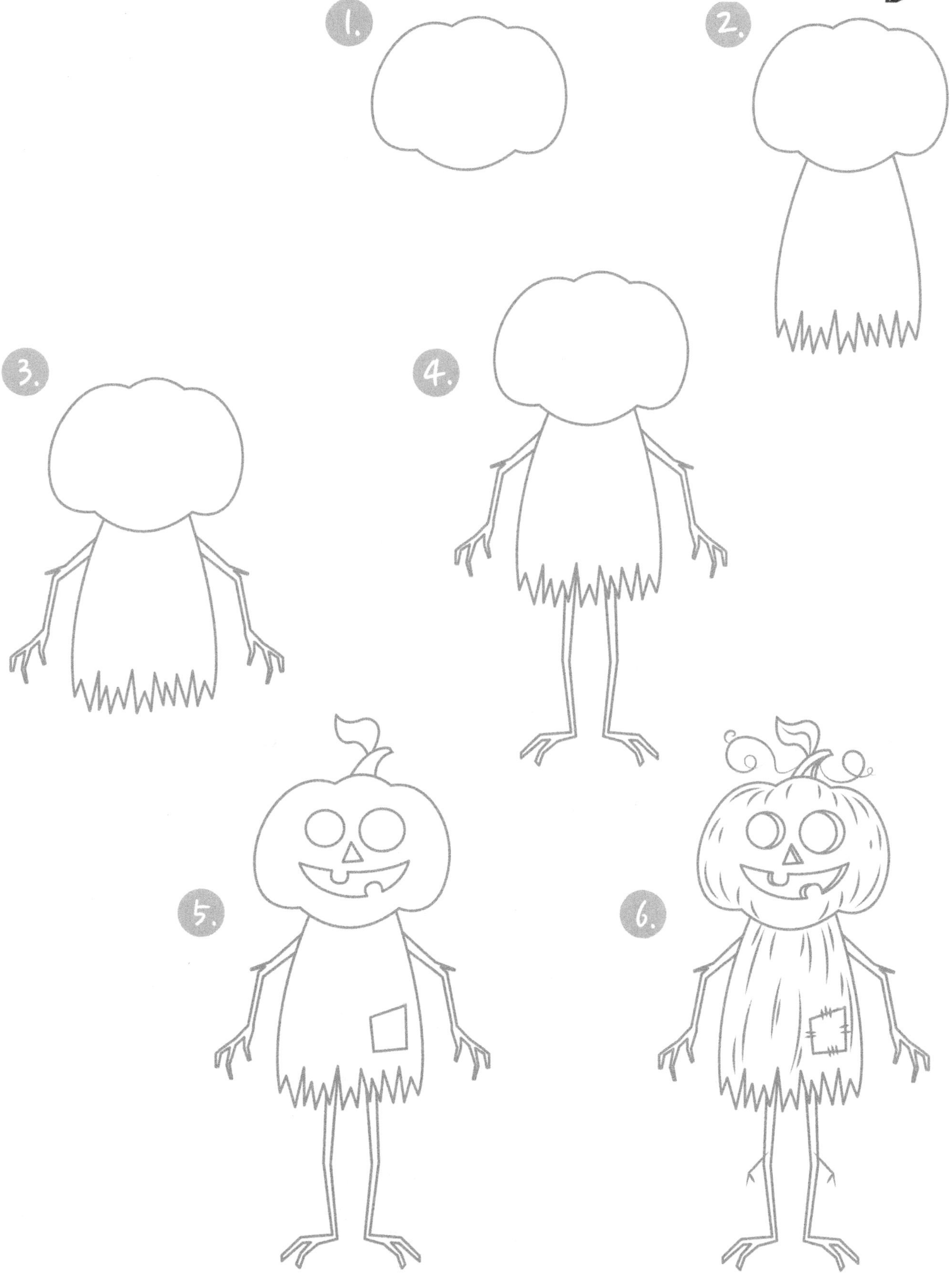

BAT

1

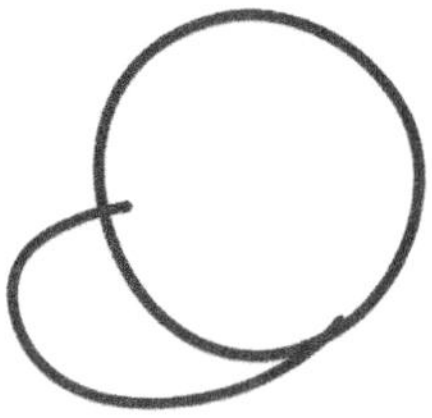

2

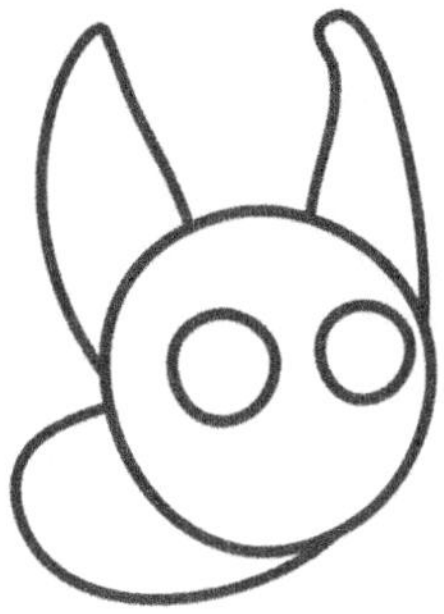

3

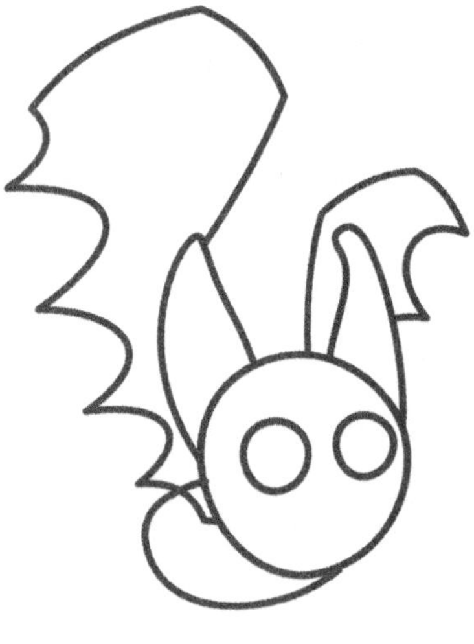

4

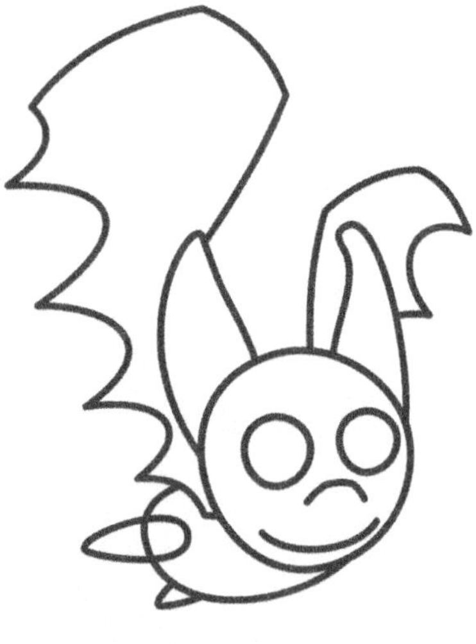

5

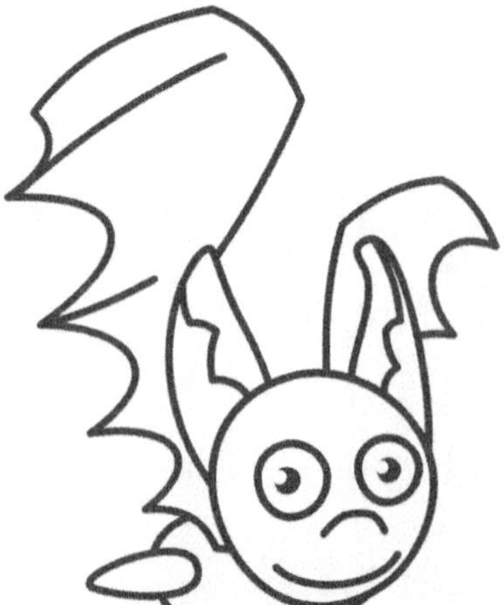

FLYING WITCH

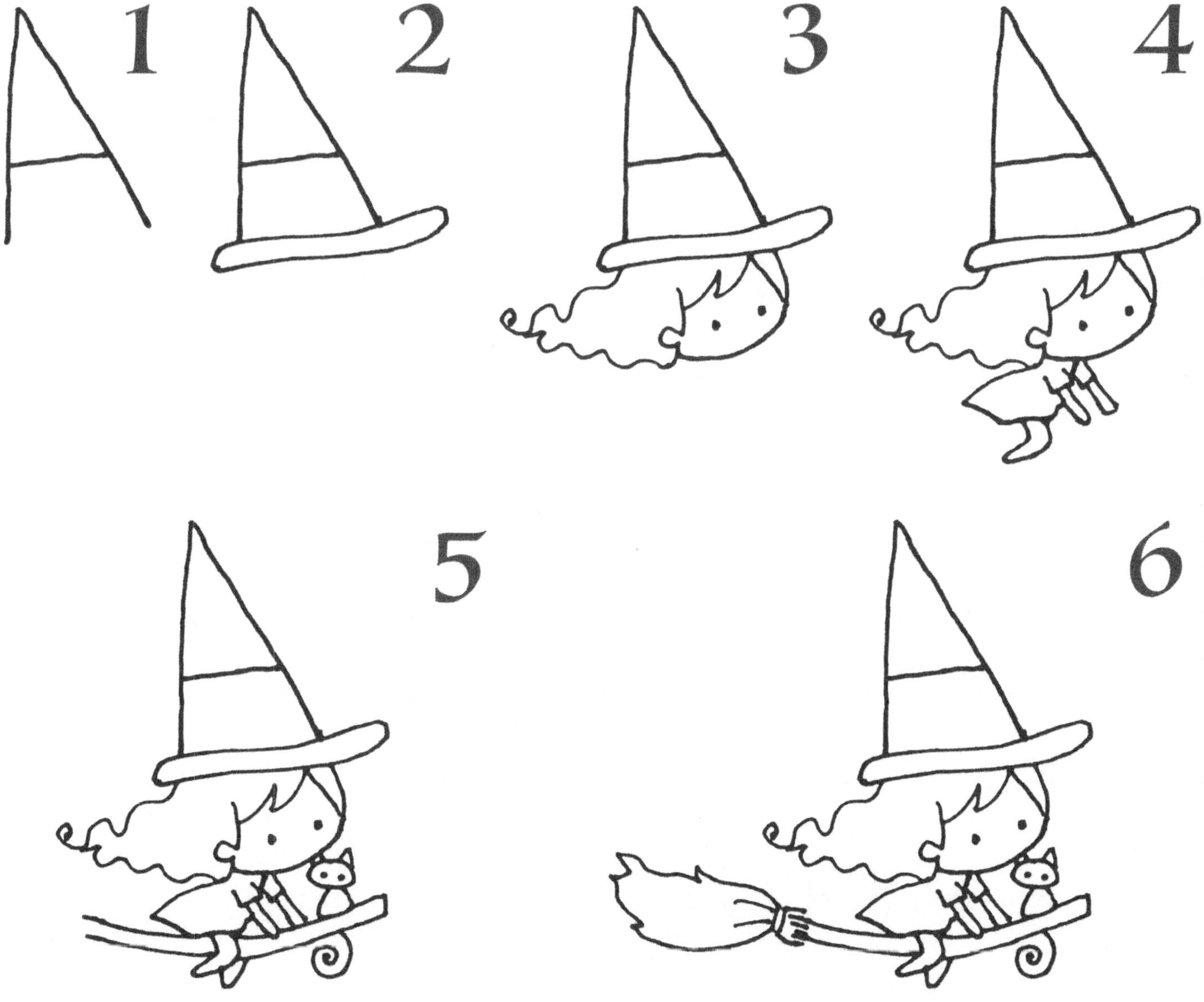

OWL

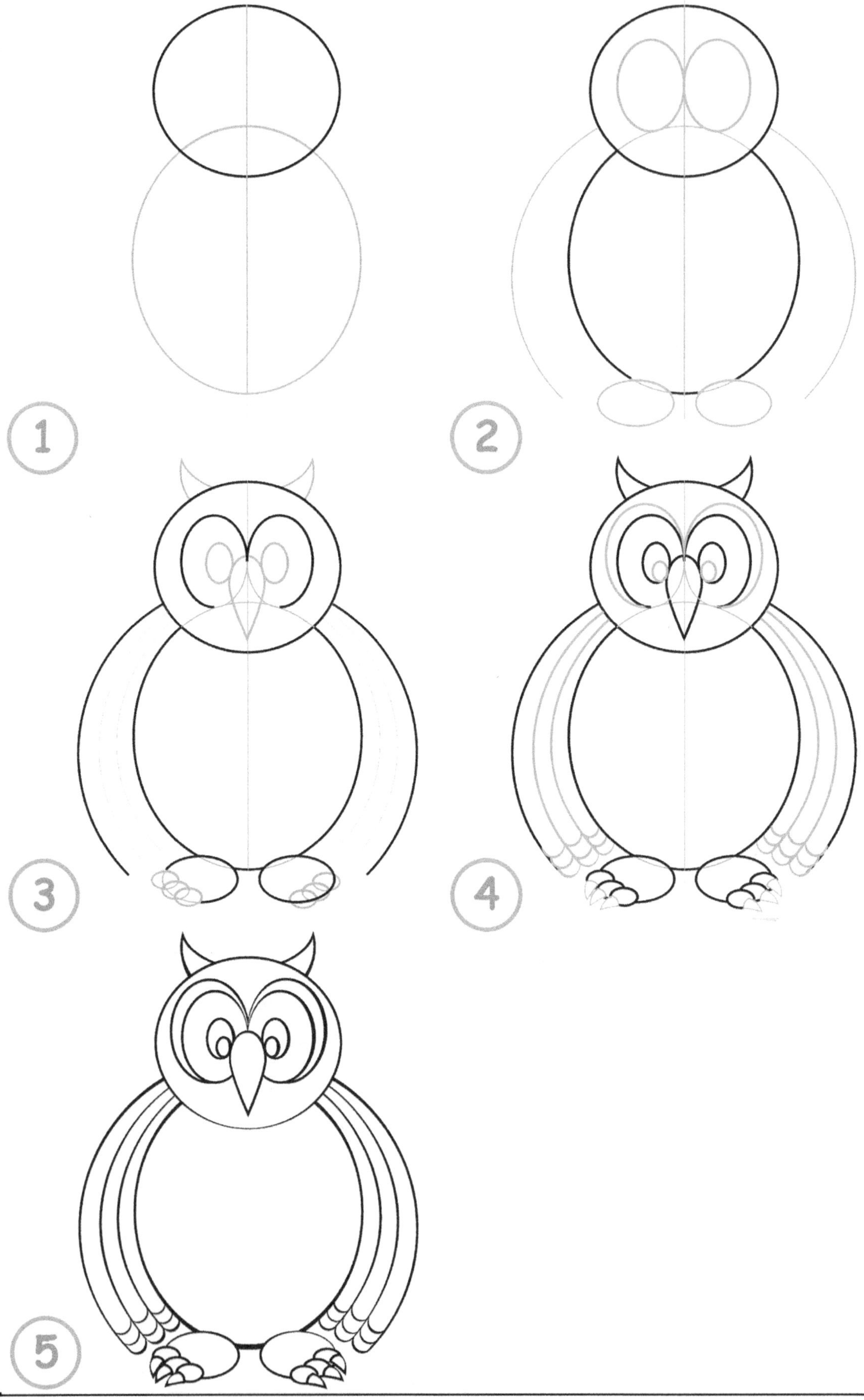

FROG

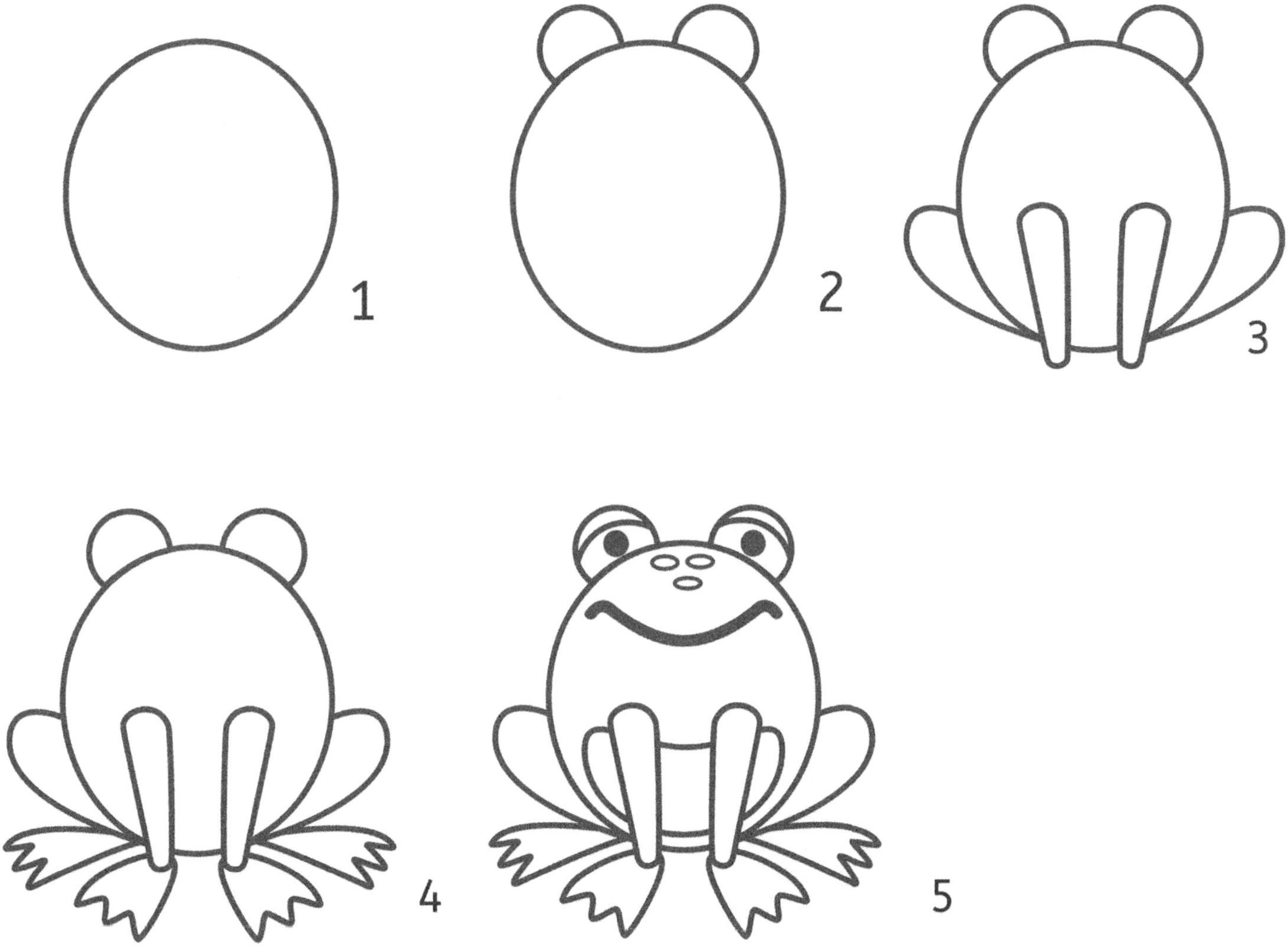

FALL LEAF

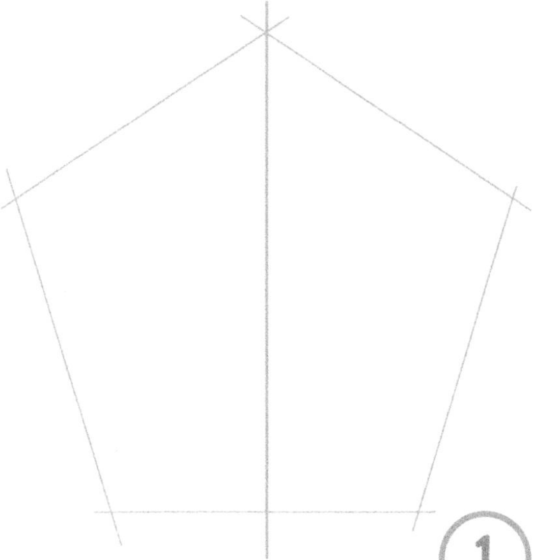

1

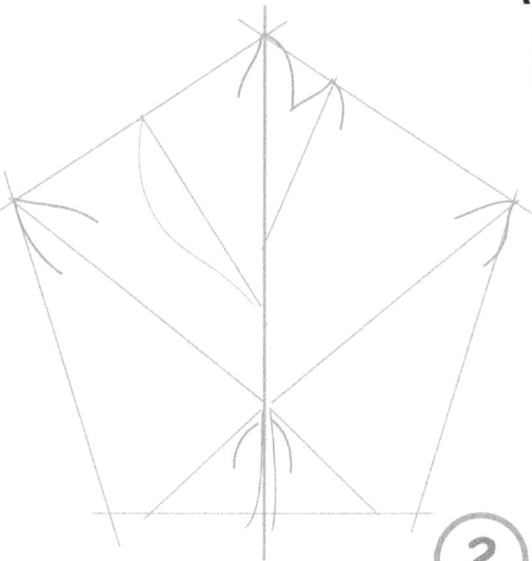

2

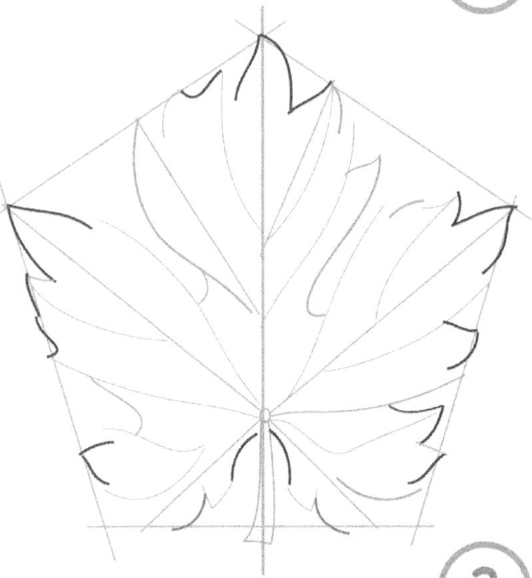

3

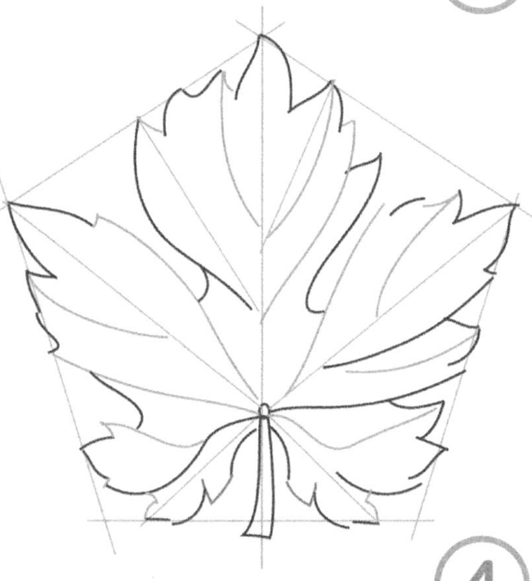

4

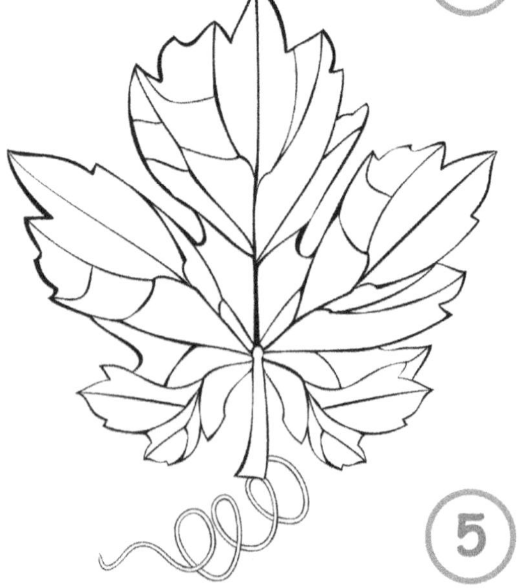

5

FLYING BAT

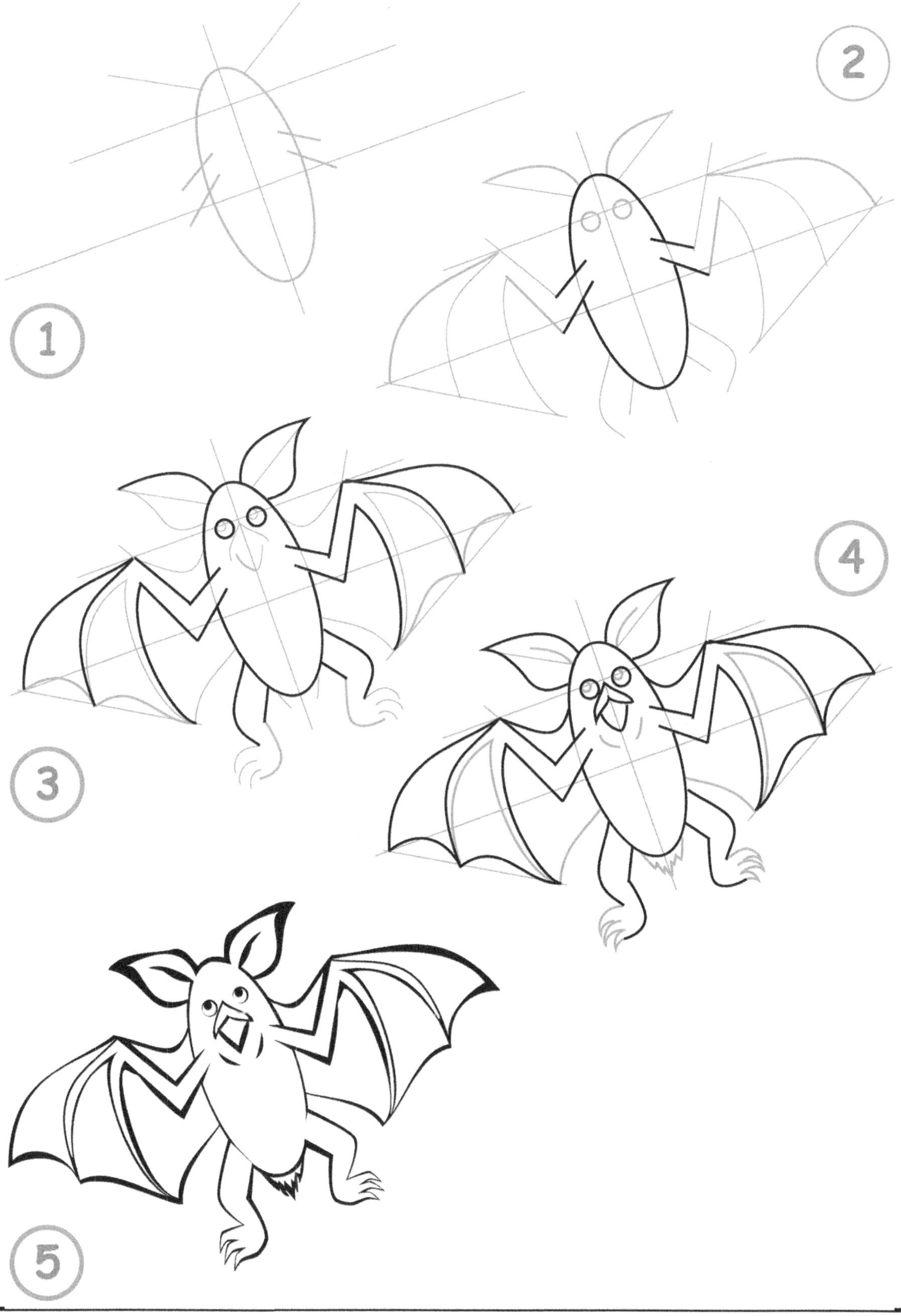

SKULL

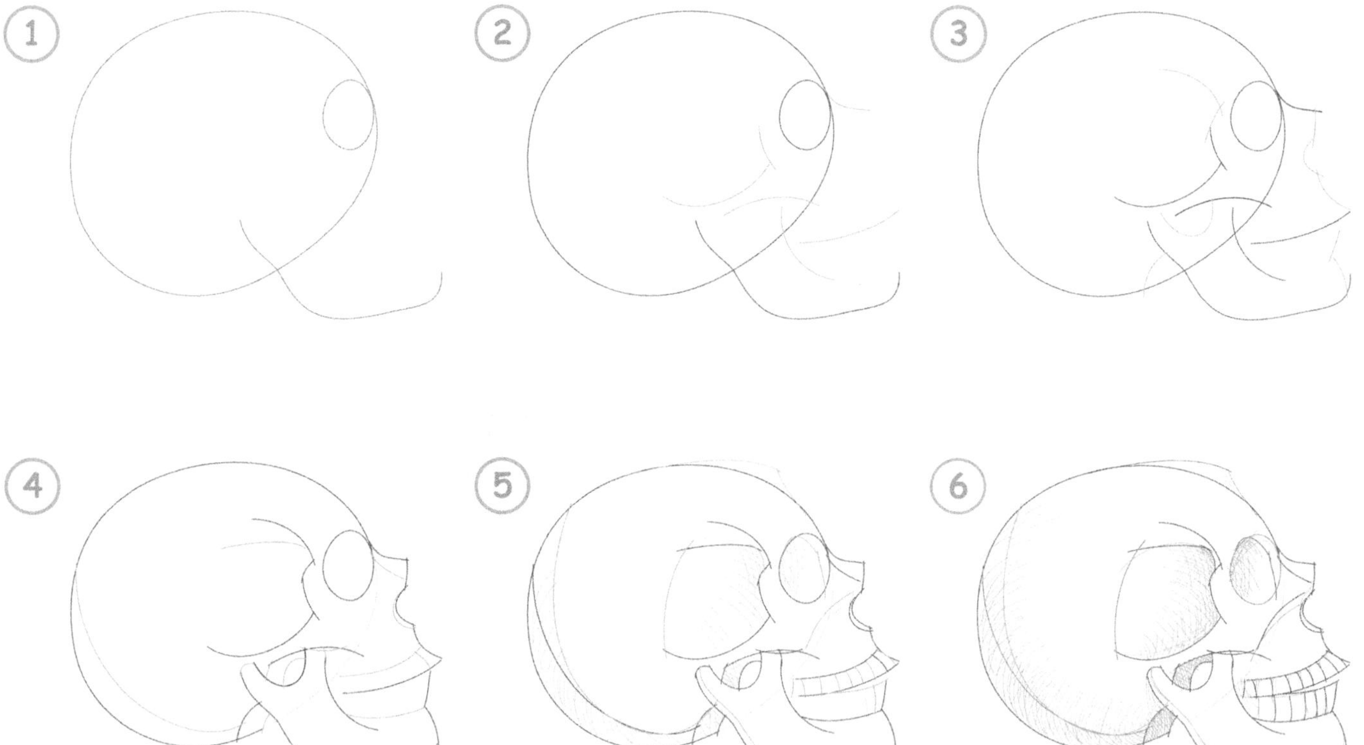

OWL

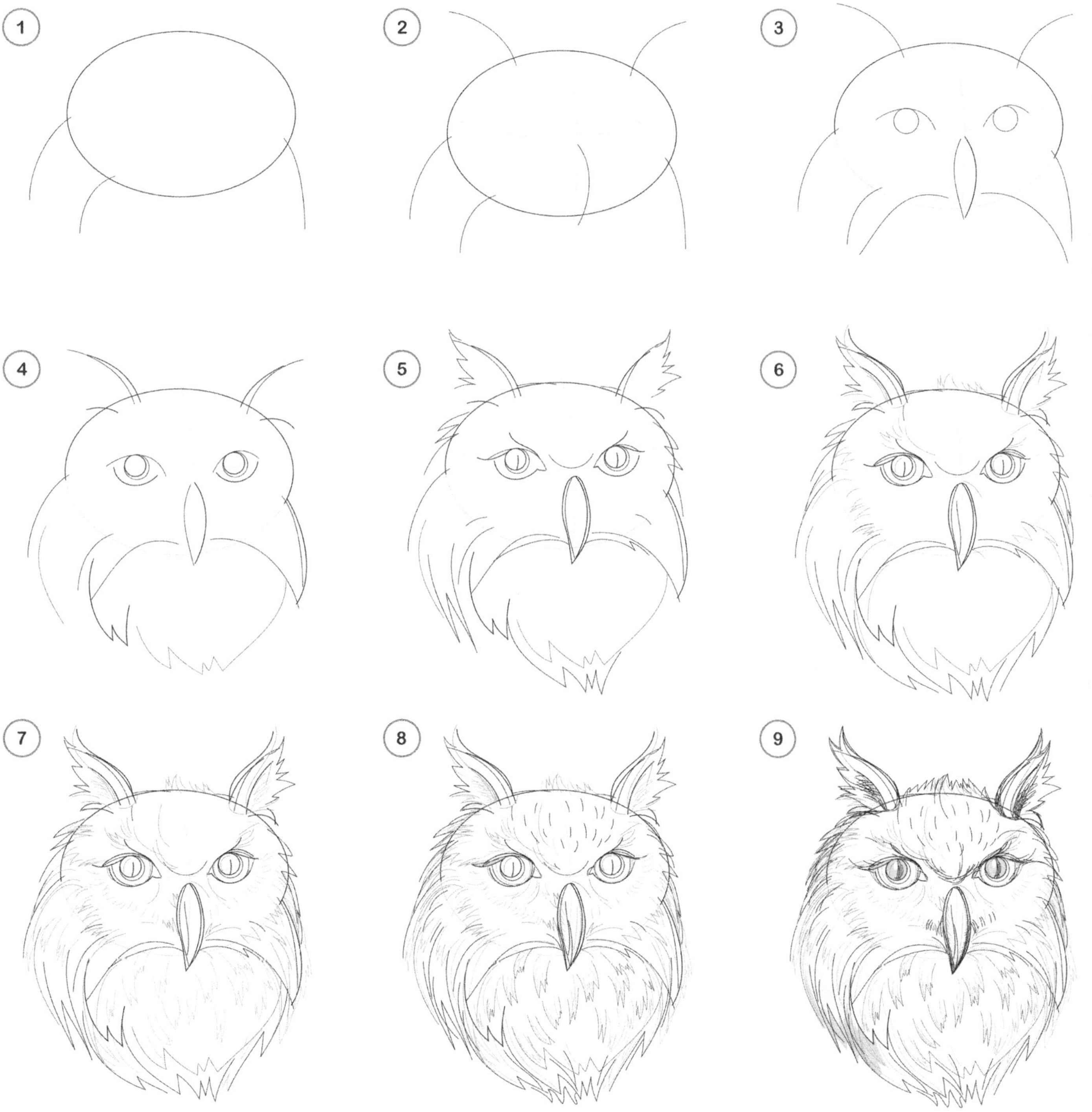

FROG

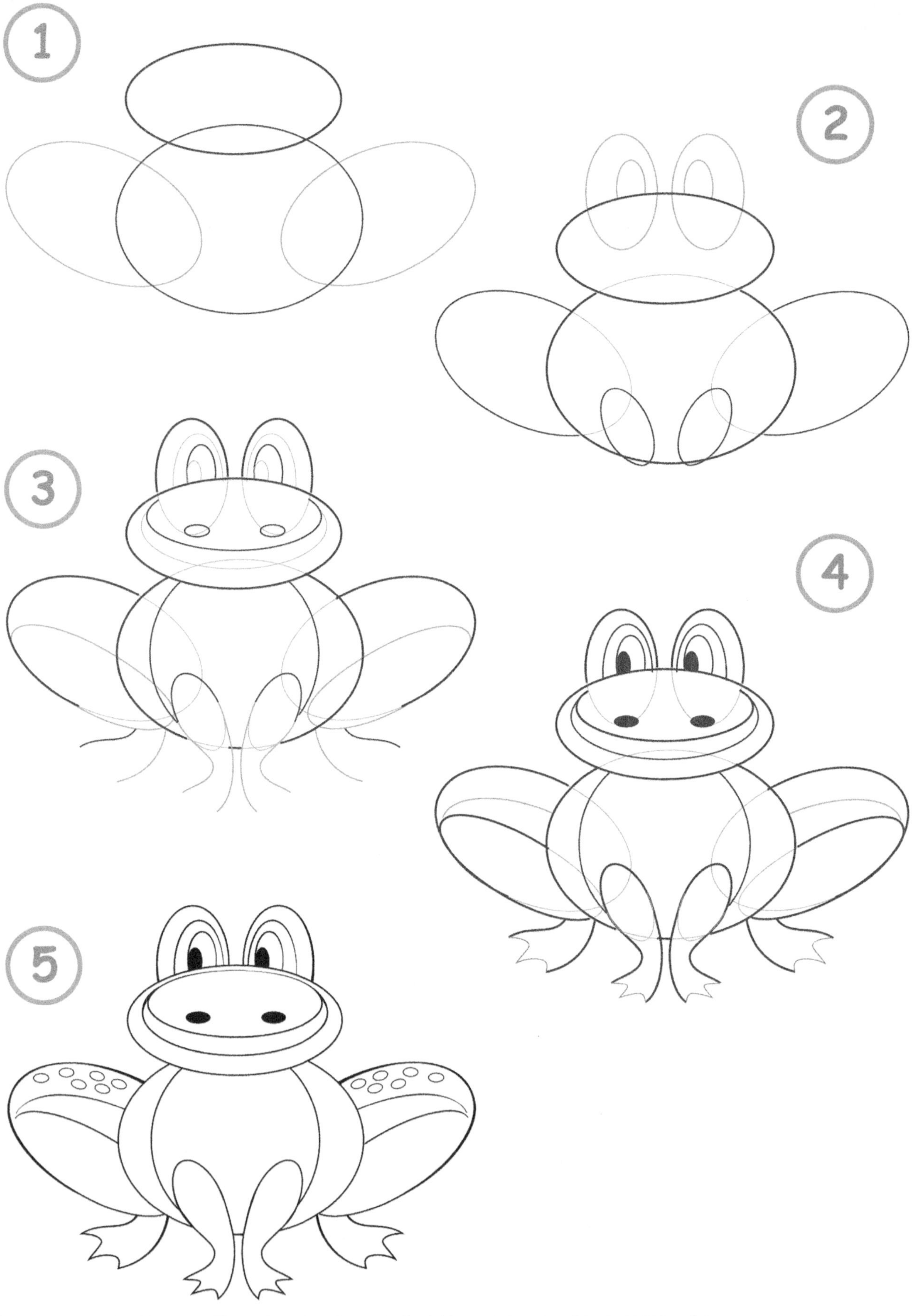

CAT

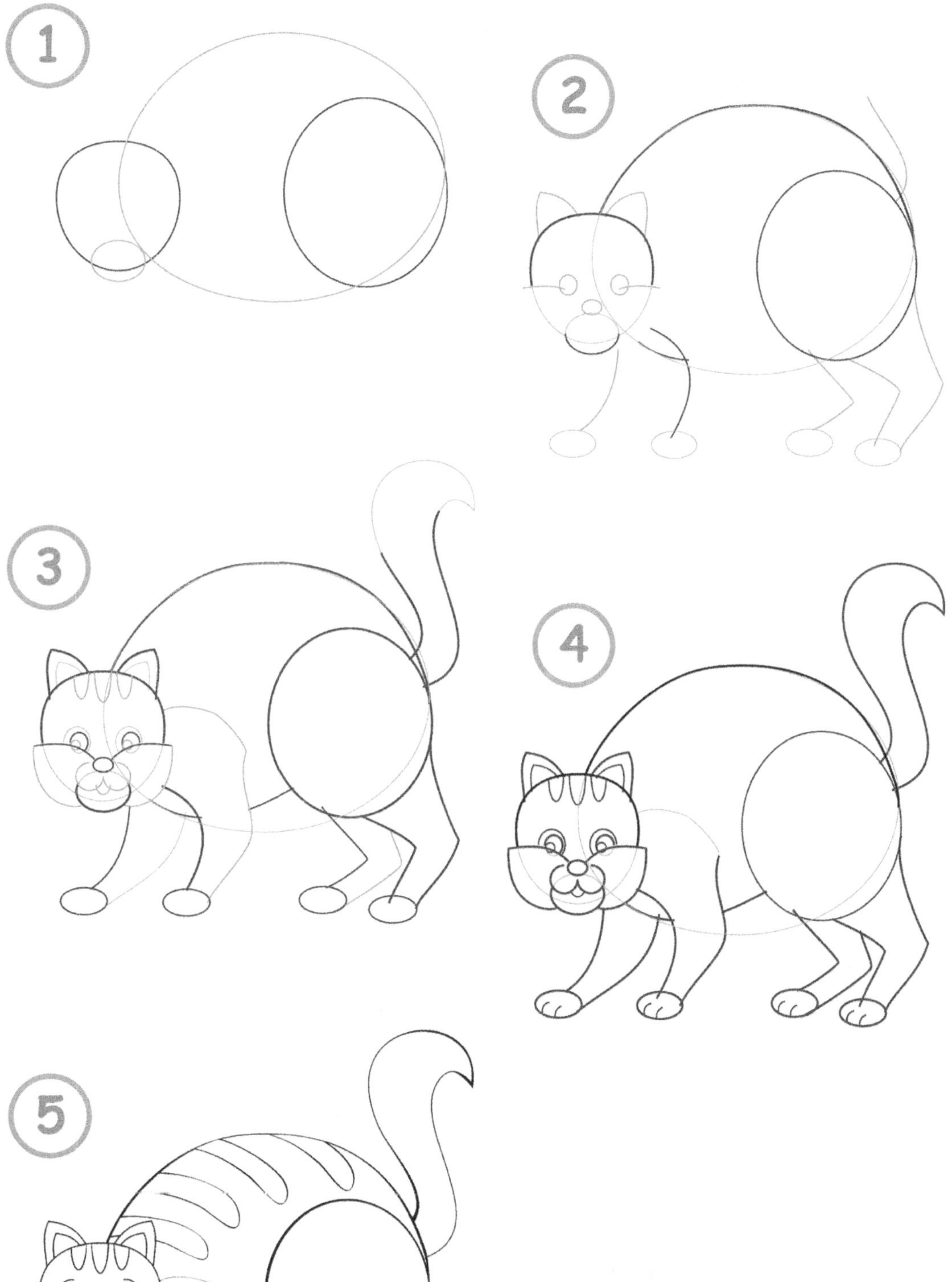

BAT

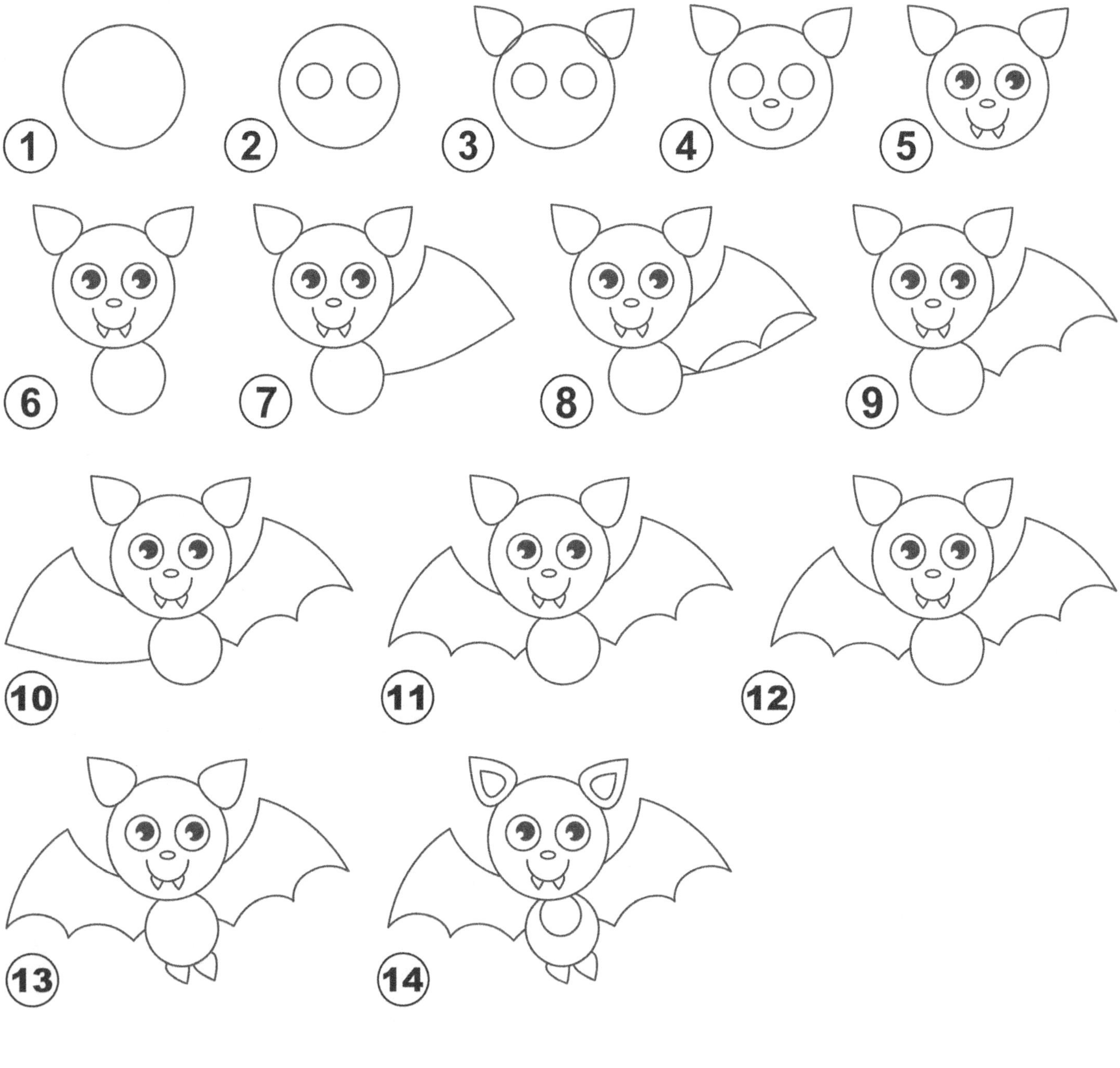

WIZARD

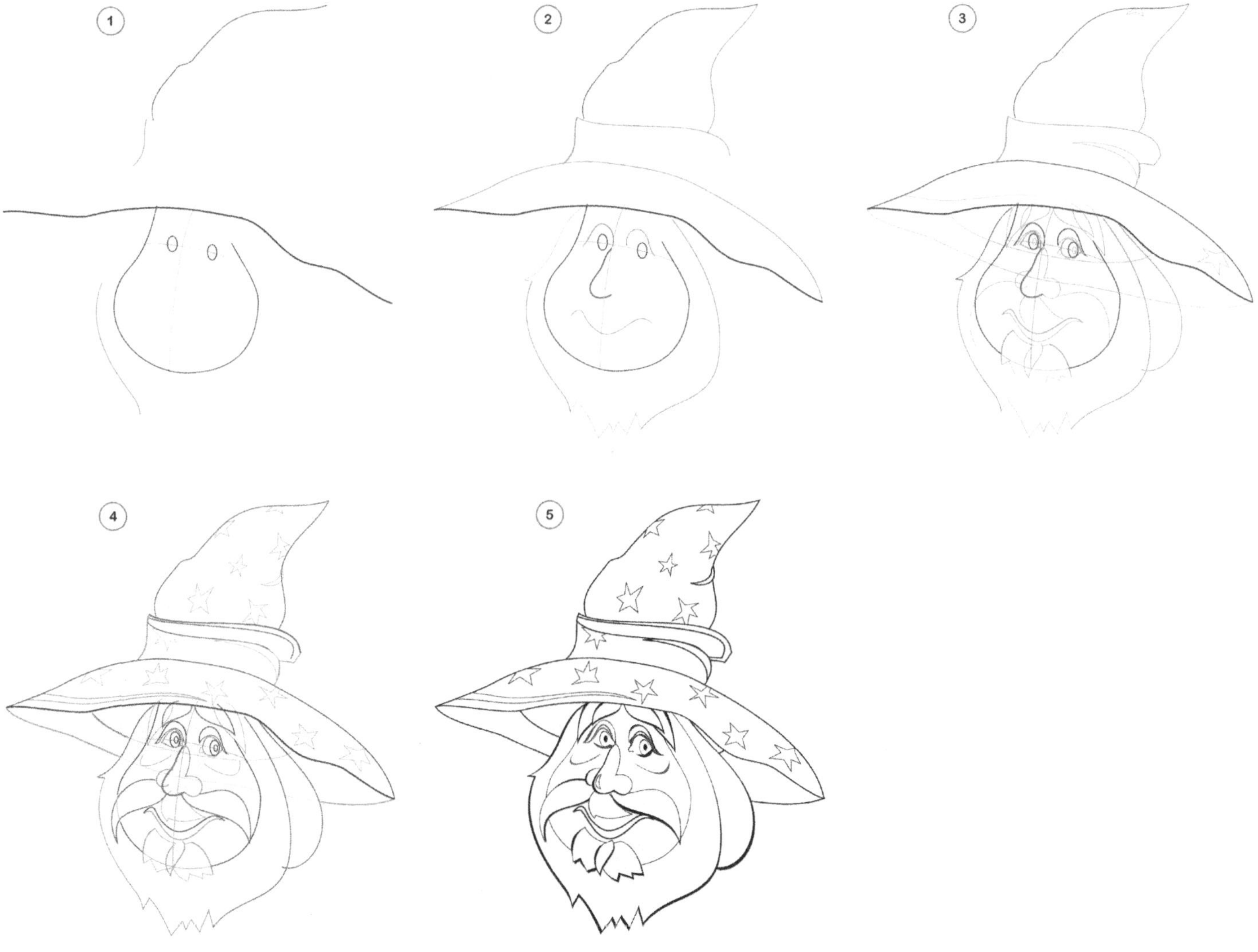

OWL

1.

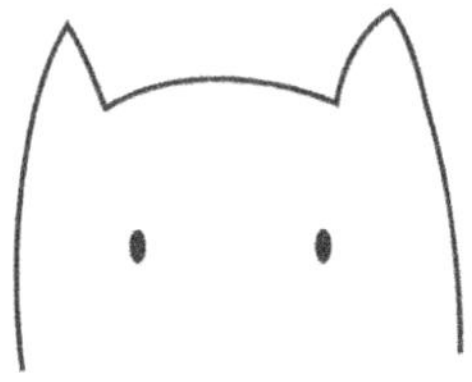

2.

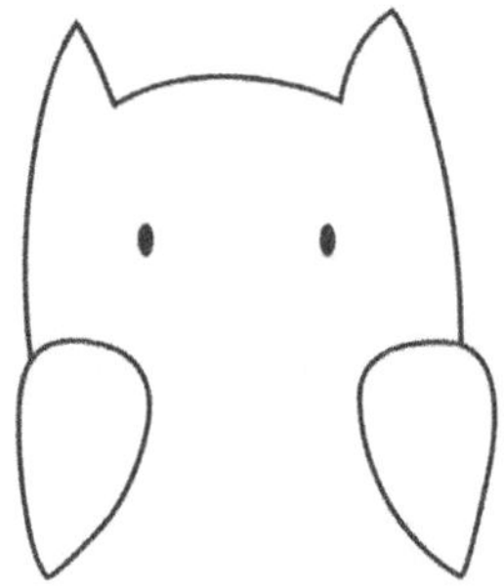

3.

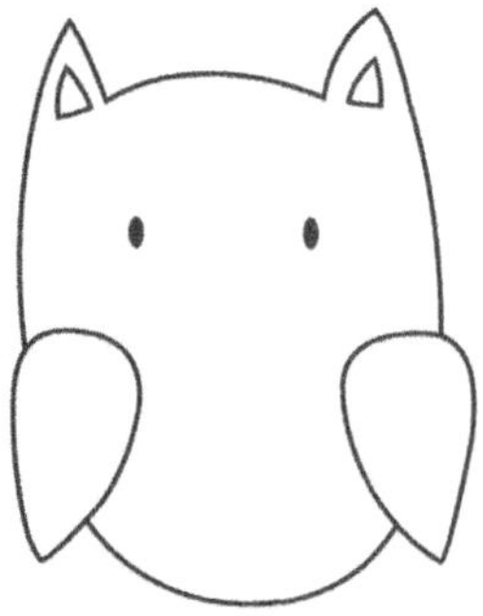

4.

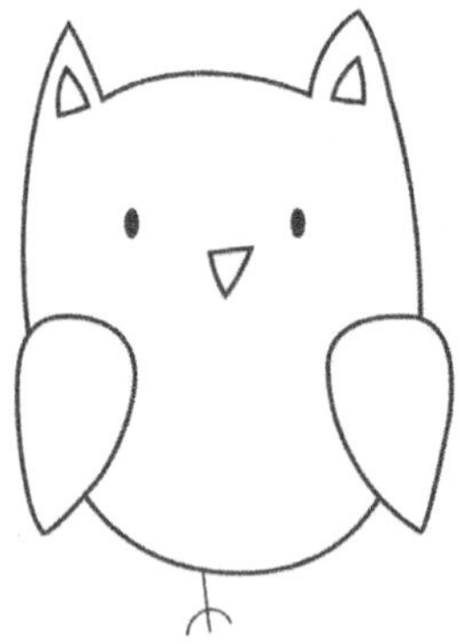

5.

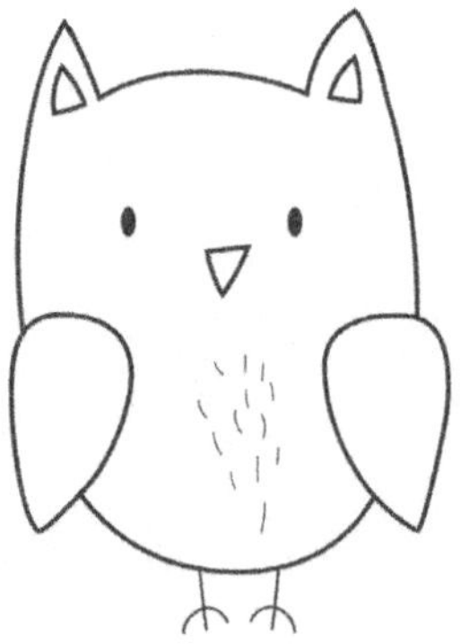

CUTE MONSTER

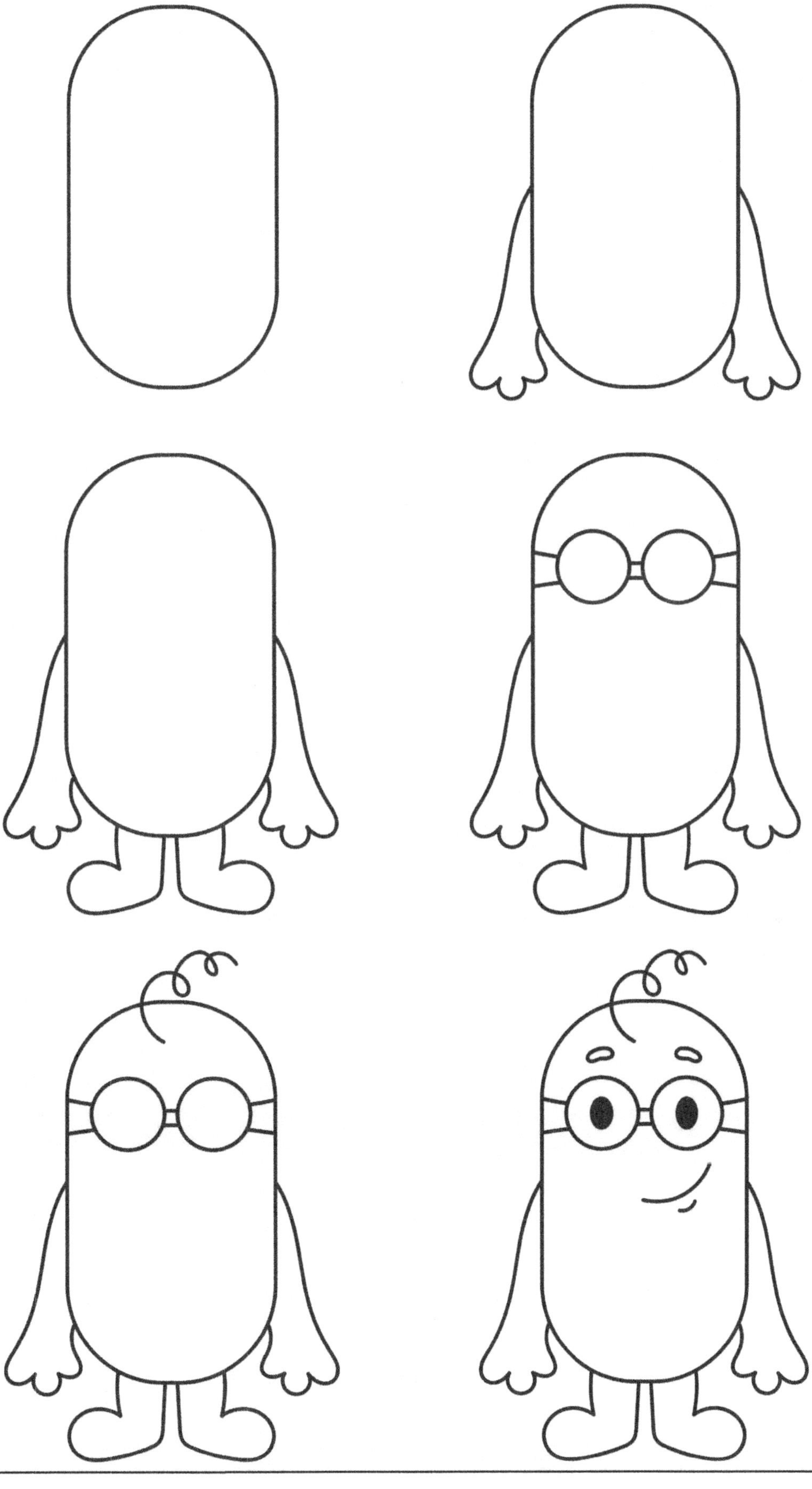

CANDLE

1.

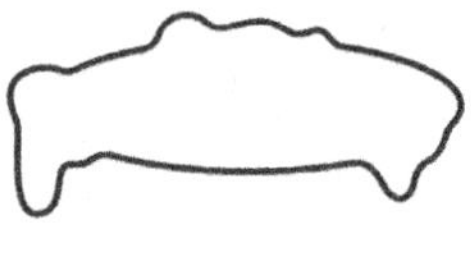

2.

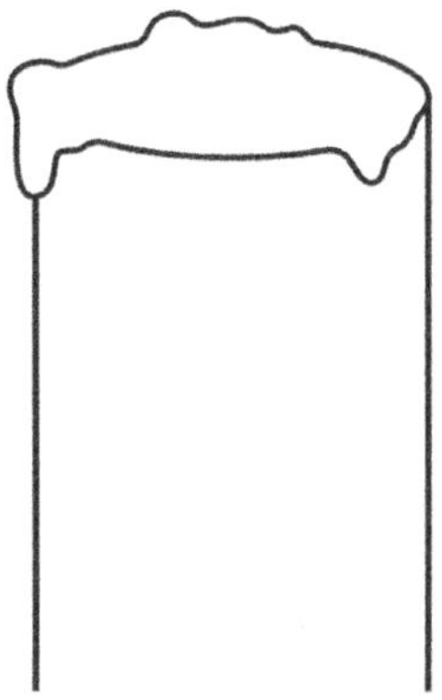

3.

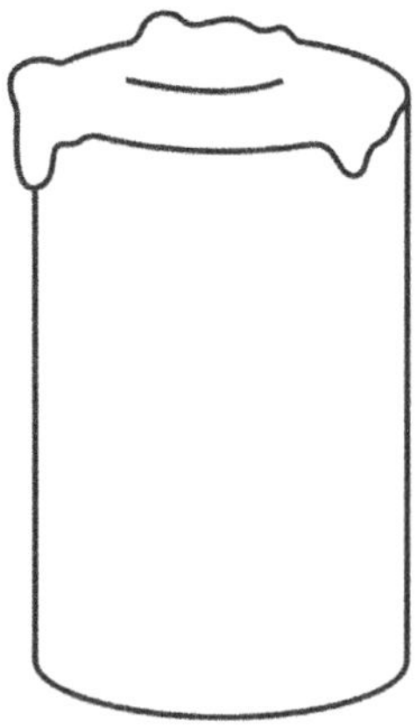

4.

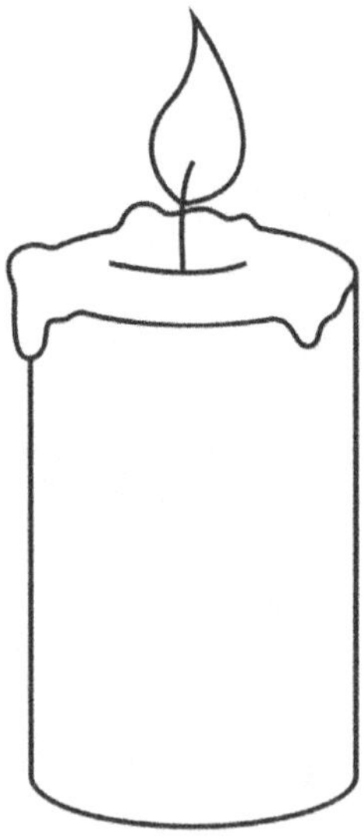

PUMPKIN

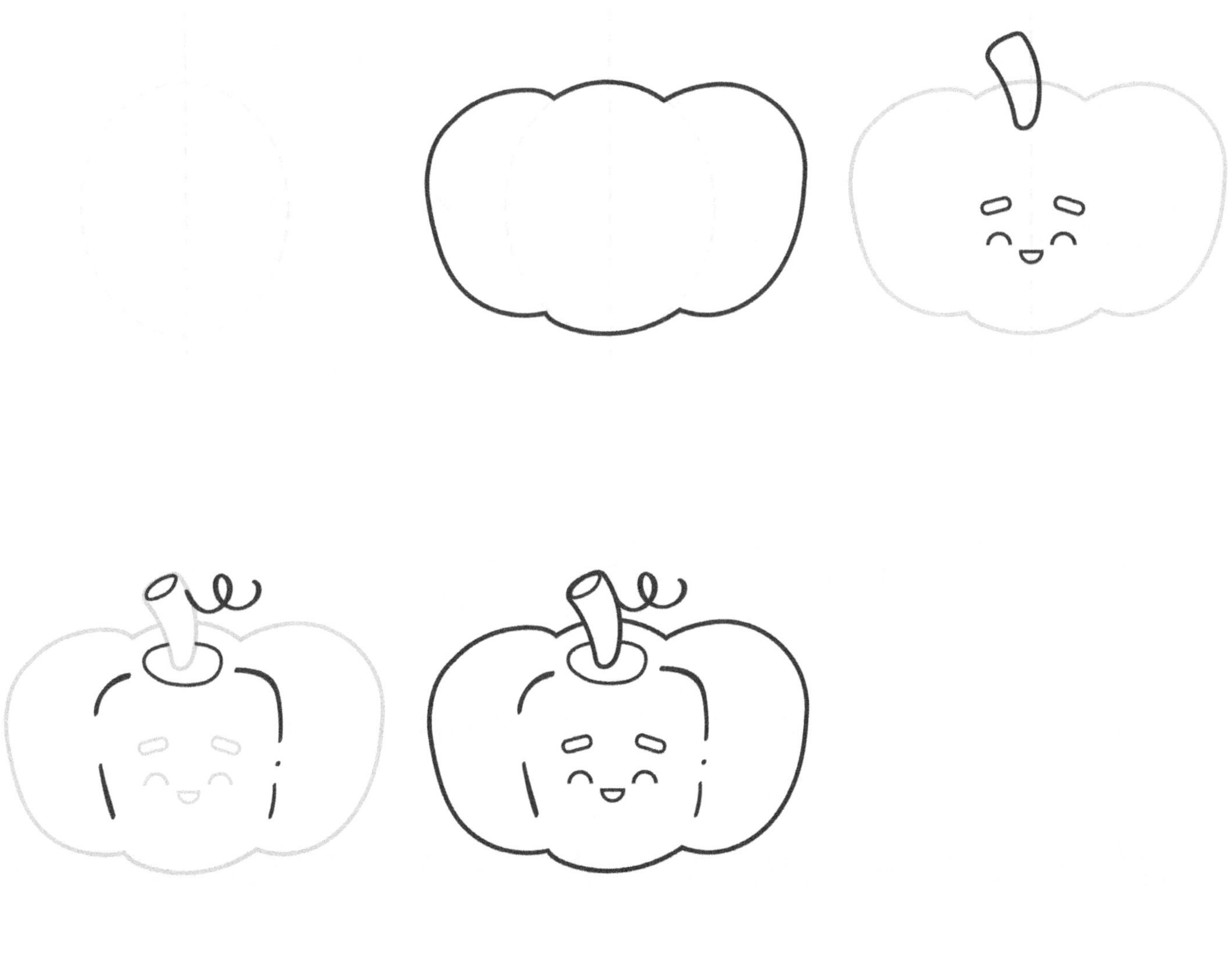

TREE

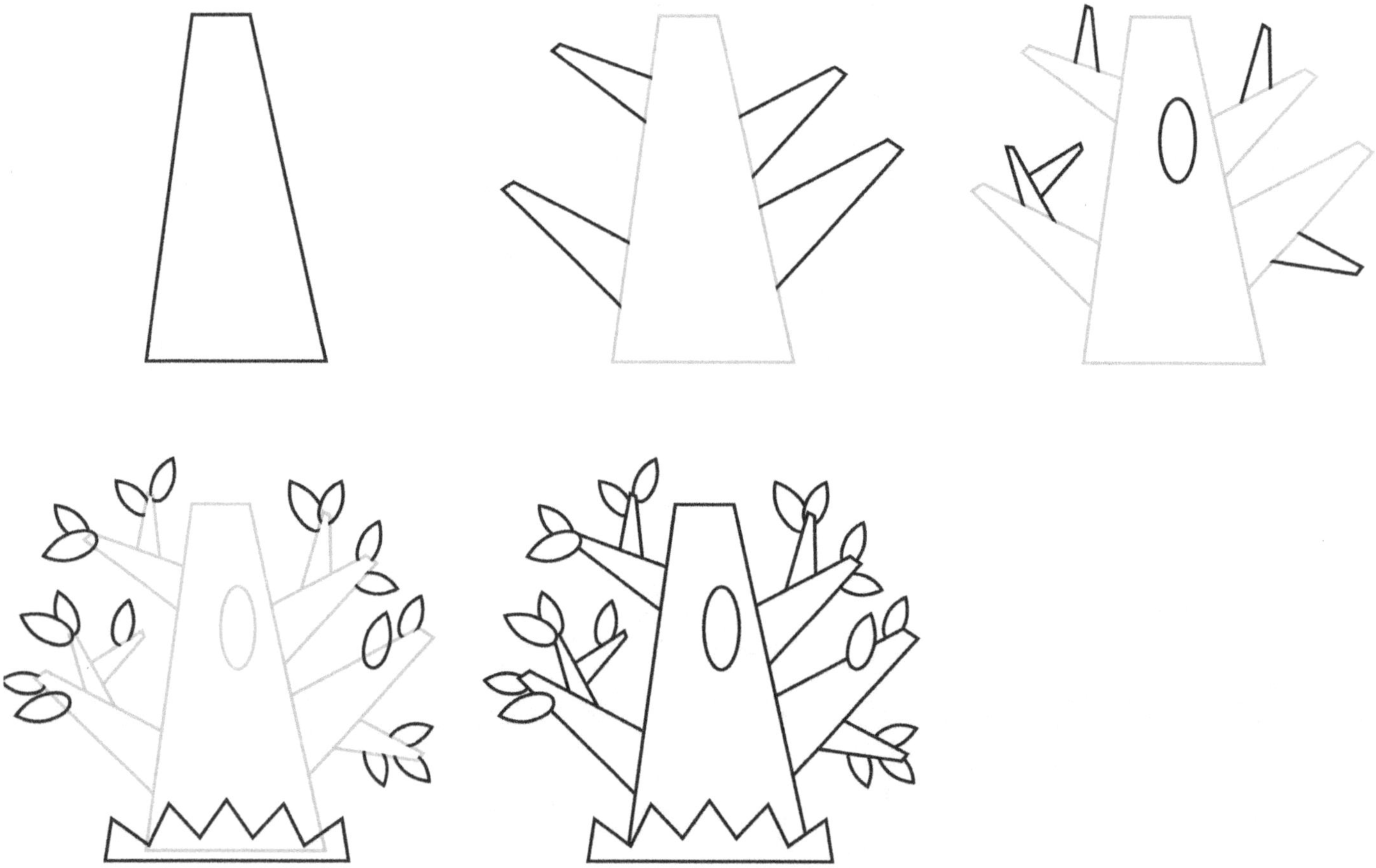

FAIRY

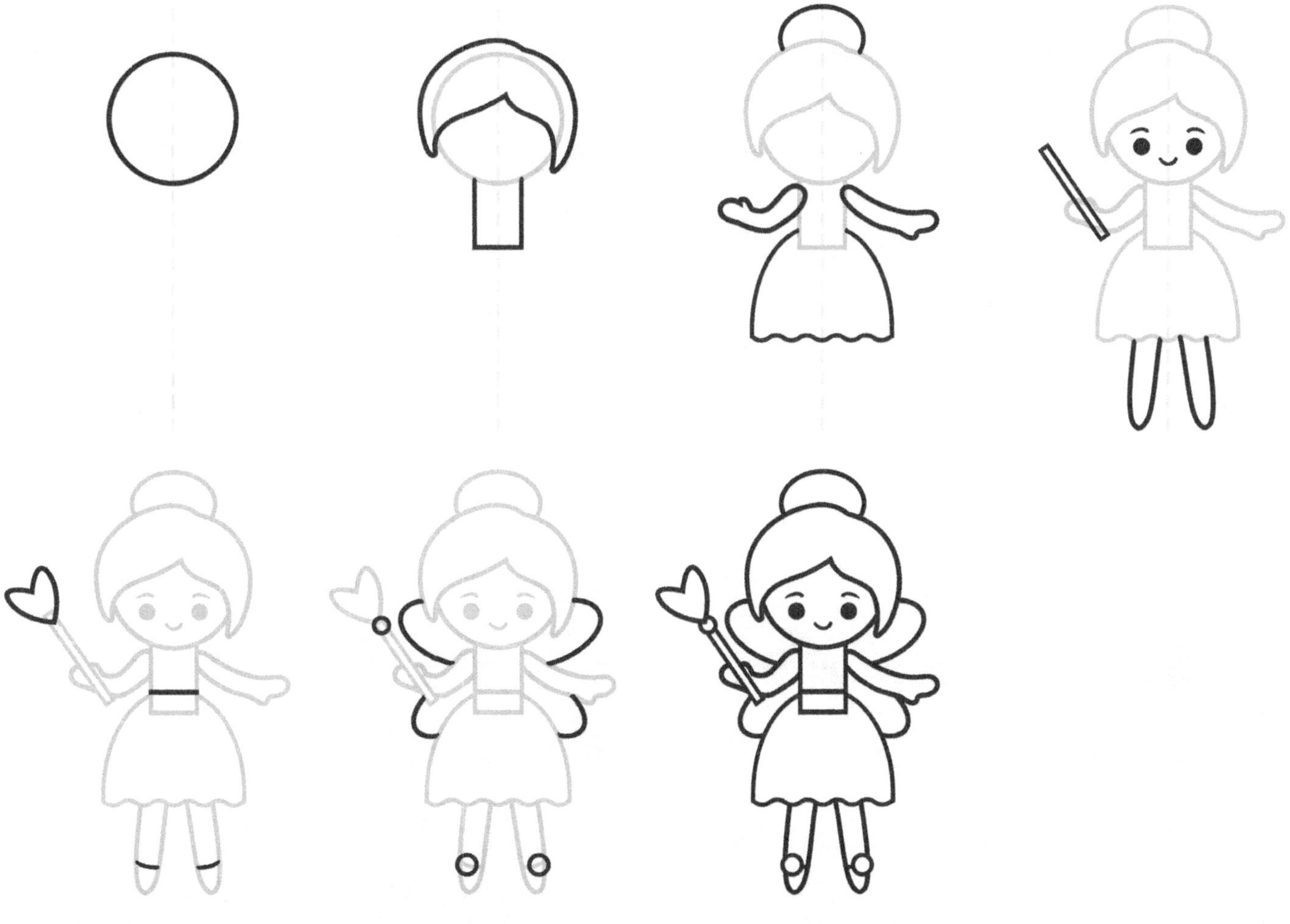

PIRATE

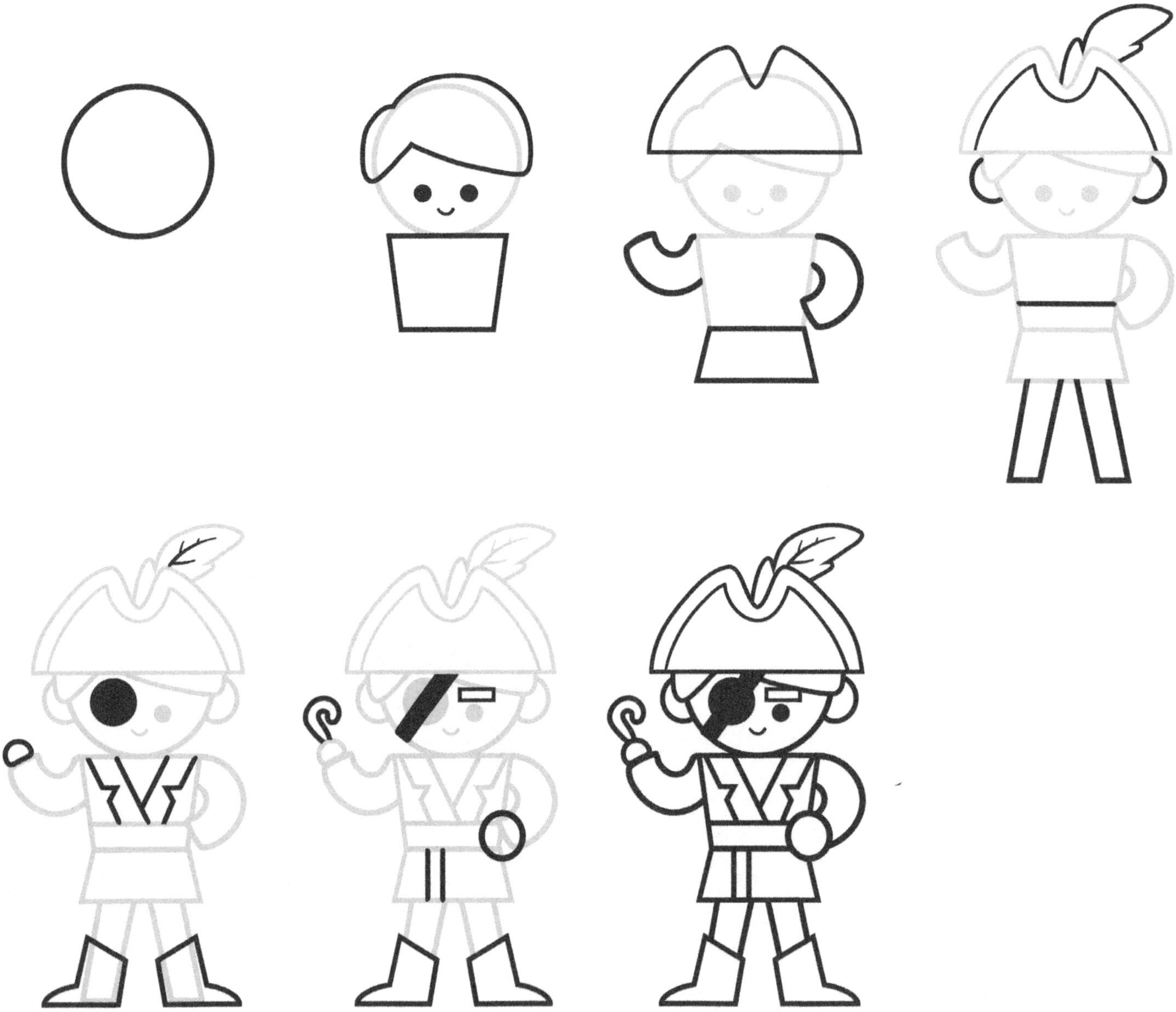

HAPPY SPIDER

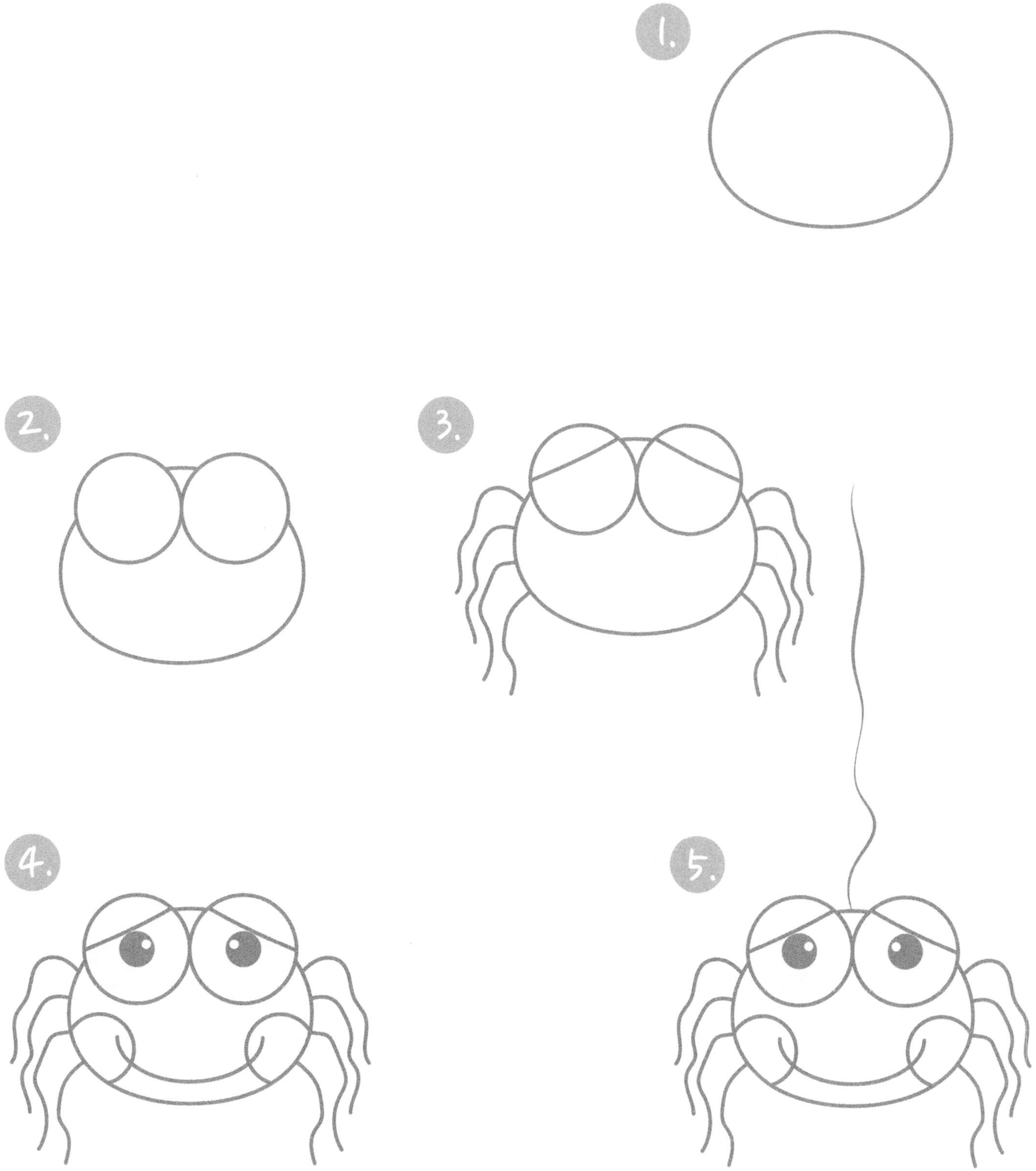

CANDY BUCKET

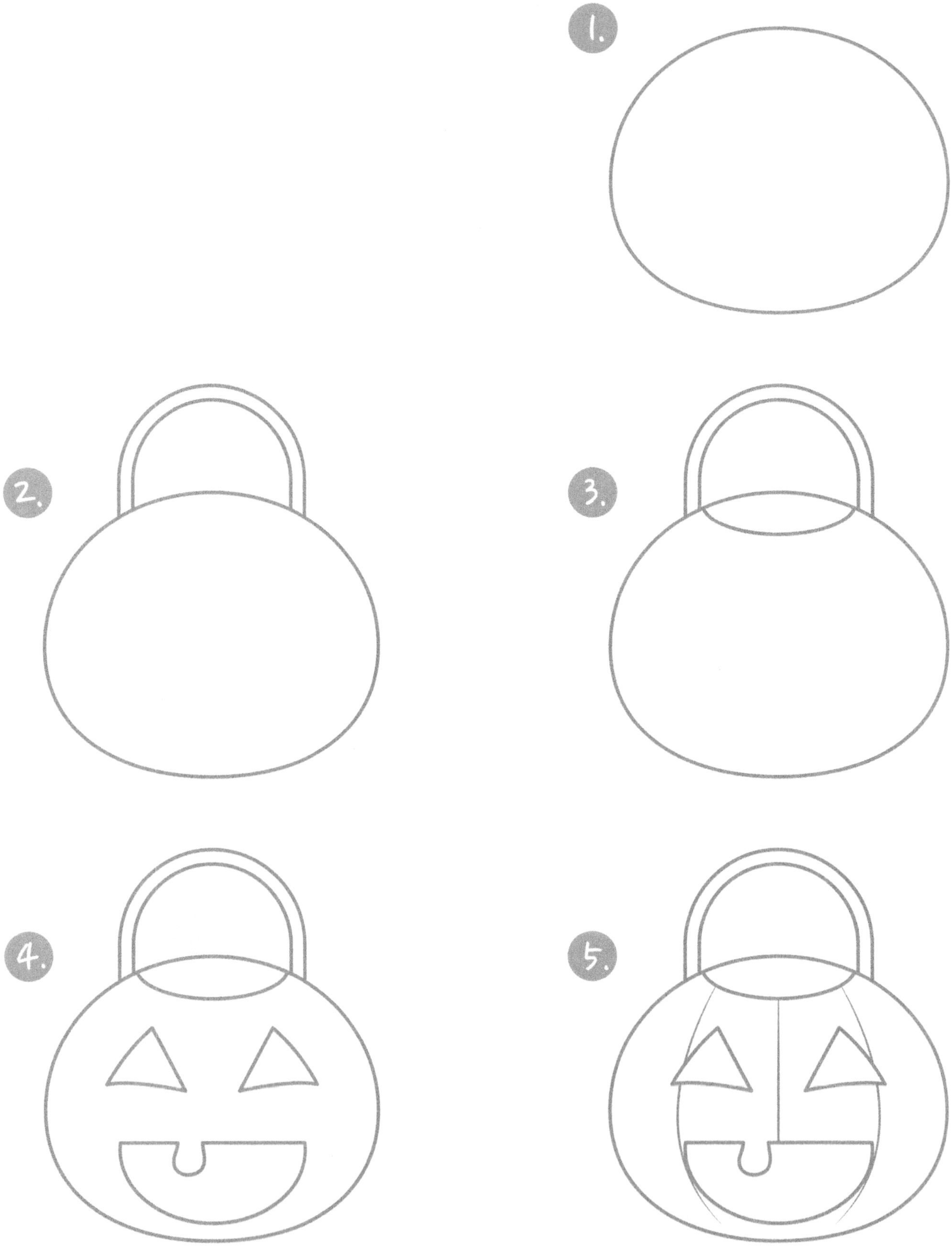

PUMPKIN

1.

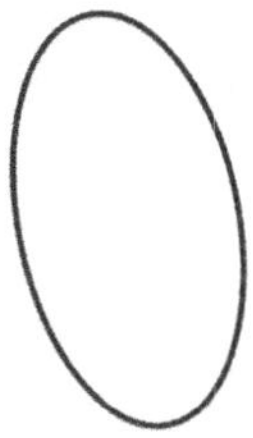

2.

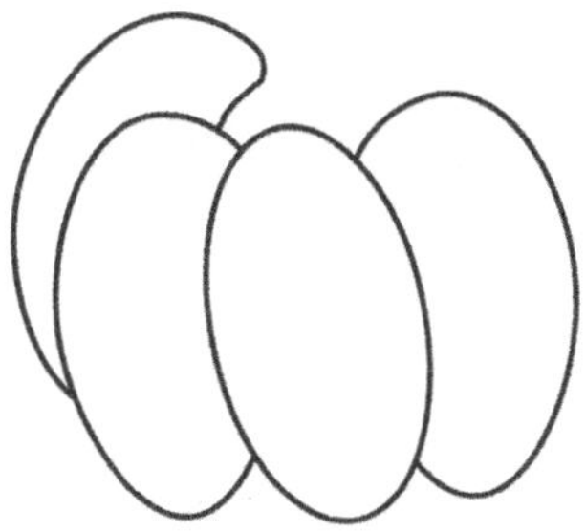

3.

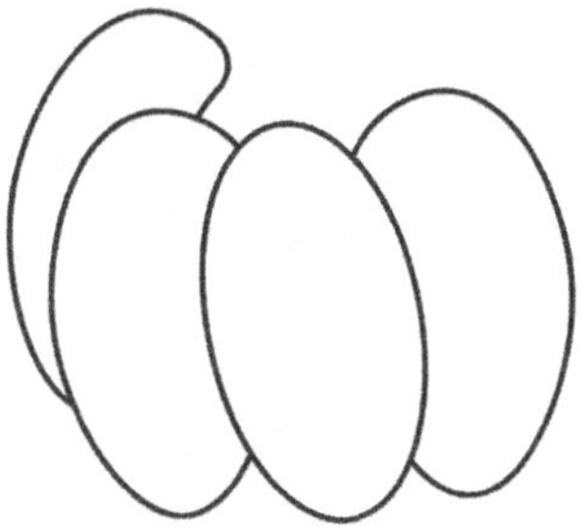

4.

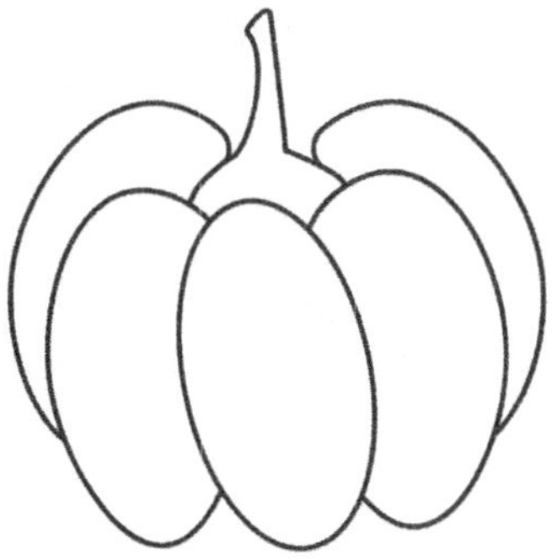

5.

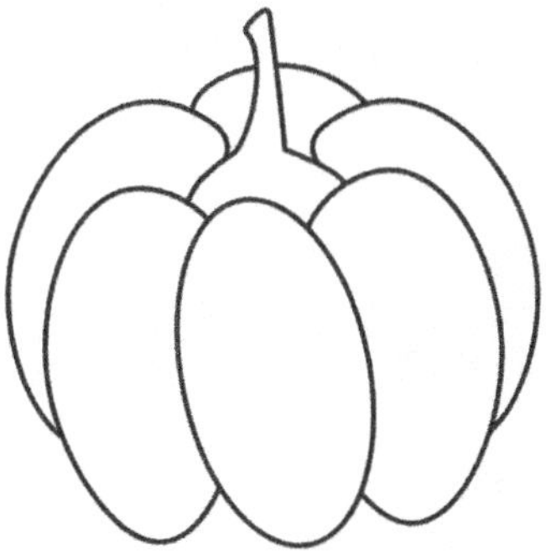

FALLING LEAF

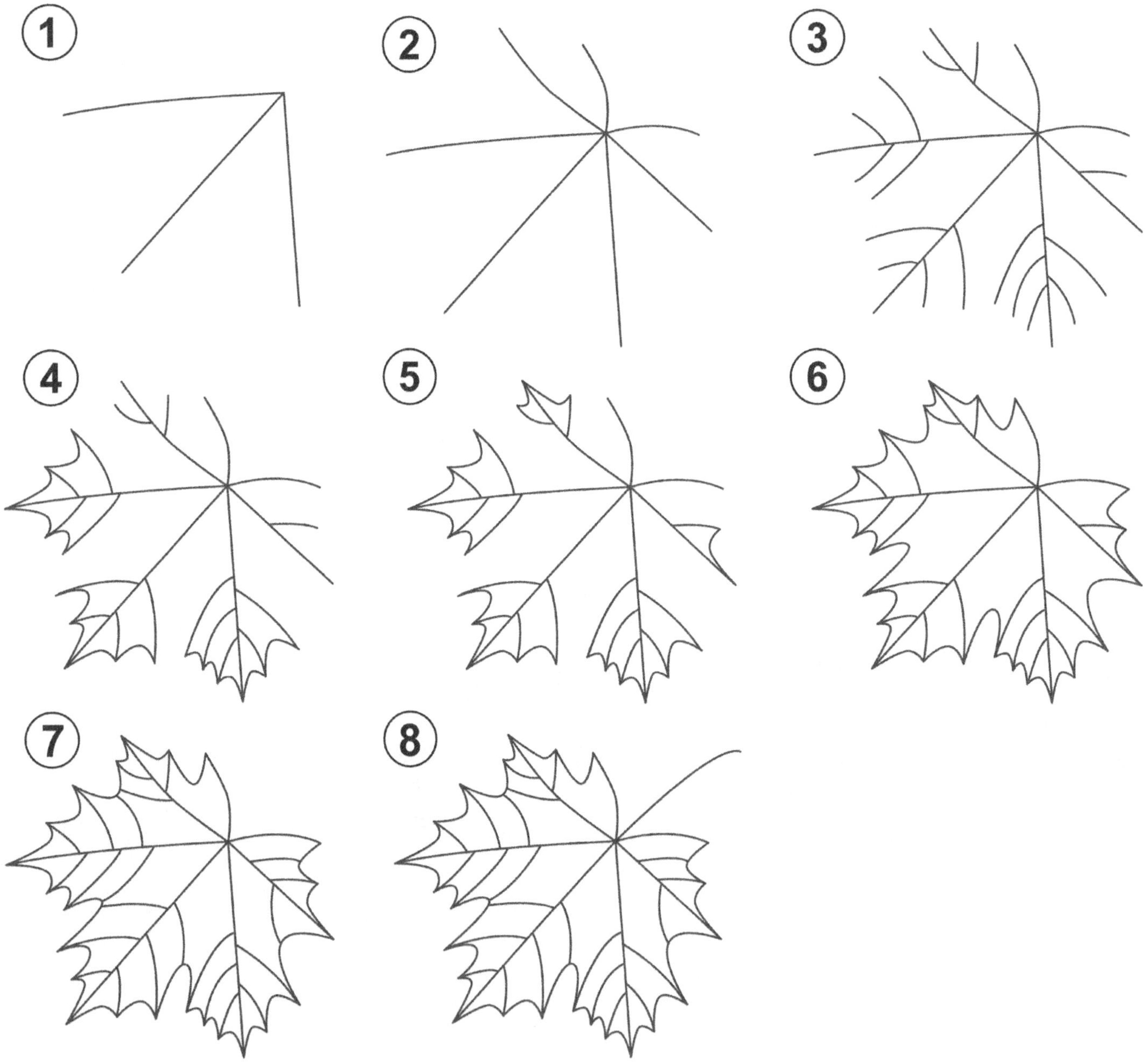

GOOGLY EYES

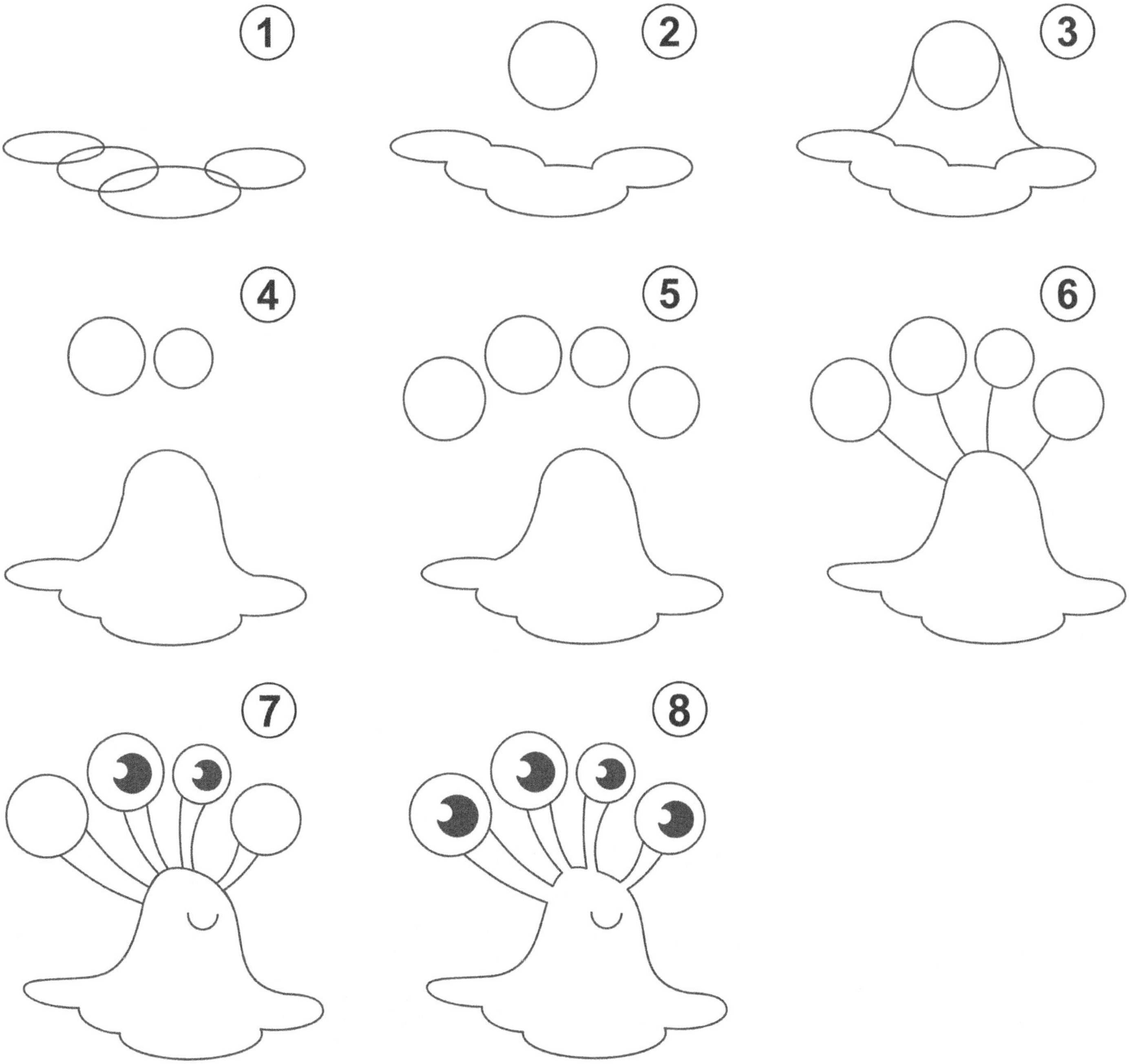

Made in the USA
Las Vegas, NV
24 October 2024

10402130R00031